Human Growth & DEVELOPMENT

CLEP* Test Study Guide

All rights reserved. This Study Guide, Book and Flashcards are protected under the US Copyright Law. No part of this book or study guide or flashcards may be reproduced, distributed or stored in a retrieval system, or transmitted in any form or by any means, electronic, mechanical, photocopying, recording, or otherwise, without the prior written permission of the publisher Breely Crush Publishing, LLC.

© 2020 Breely Crush Publishing, LLC

*CLEP is a registered trademark of the College Entrance Examination Board which does not endorse this book.

971010420143

Copyright ©2003 - 2020, Breely Crush Publishing, LLC.

All rights reserved.

This Study Guide, Book and Flashcards are protected under the US Copyright Law. No part of this publication may be reproduced, distributed or stored in a retrieval system, or transmitted in any form or by any means, electronic, mechanical, photocopying, recording, or otherwise, without the prior written permission of the publisher Breely Crush Publishing, LLC.

Published by Breely Crush Publishing, LLC
10808 River Front Parkway
South Jordan, UT 84095
www.breelycrushpublishing.com

ISBN-10: 1-61433-637-7
ISBN-13: 978-1-61433-637-2

Printed and bound in the United States of America.

*CLEP is a registered trademark of the College Entrance Examination Board which does not endorse this book.

Table of Contents

Introduction 1
Erikson's Developmental Stages 1
Jean Piaget 2
Piaget's Relevant Definitions 3
Piaget's Stages of Development 4
Freud's Psychosexual Stages 6
Defense Mechanisms 7
Maslow's Hierarchy of Needs 8
Classical Conditioning 8
Operant Conditioning 9
Reinforcers 9
Behavior 10
Social Learning Theory 10
Language Development 11
Fast Mapping 11
Conducting Studies 12
Human Biology 17
Development After Birth 19
Adolescence 21
IQ Testing 22
Language Development 23
Id, Ego and Super Ego 24
Child Learning 26
Kibbutz 26
Kohlberg's Theory of Moral Development 26
Childhood 27
Divorce 30
Aging 30
Sample Test Questions 31
Test-Taking Strategies 60
What Your Score Means 60
Test Preparation 61
Suffix 1 62
Legal Note 66
References 66

Introduction

Congratulations! You've bought and are reading the best resource to passing your Human Growth and Development CLEP test. CLEP tests are a great way to save time and money. If you learn the contents of this study guide, passing the test should not be an issue.

Erikson's Developmental Stages

Erik Erikson was a psychoanalyst who created stages of emotional growth in regards to human babies. Each stage has different needs and lessons to be learned. If the child or infant does not learn that lesson, he may have a harder time in life down the road. For example, if a baby is crying constantly and is not taken care of, or if it is ignored, it can come to feel mistrust toward others. Another example is the young adult stage. The young adult must deal with either being intimate with someone or deal with feeling isolated. According to Erikson, the most important thing is the development of trust.

Infant — *Trust vs. Mistrust*
Infants gain trust and confidence from their caregivers. If those caregivers are warm and responsive then they will know that the world is good.

Toddler — *Autonomy vs. Shame and Doubt*
Children want to choose and decide things for themselves. Autonomy is when the parents give the child that necessary free reign over their choices.

Preschooler — *Initiative vs. Guilt*
By playing make-believe the child discovers who they are and who they can become. They can try their hand at being a princess or a mother or father to their dolls.

School-Age Child — *Industry vs. Inferiority*
Children learn to work and get along with each other. Inferiority develops from negative social situations.

Adolescent — *Identity vs. Role Confusion*
The adolescent tries many roles to answer the question "Who am I?" and "Where do I fit in society?"

Young Adult — *Intimacy vs. Isolation*
Young adults work to create emotional ties and relationships to others. Because of earlier trust issues, some young adults cannot form these attachments and it leaves them isolated.

Middle-Age Adult   *Generativity vs. Stagnation*
Generativity deals with leaving something for the next generation. Those that do not do this feel an absence of accomplishment.

Old Age   *Ego Integrity vs. Despair*
In this stage, people think about the person that they have become. Integrity comes from achieving what one wanted in life. For those that are unhappy with their past, despair results in fear of death.

Jean Piaget

Jean Piaget (1896-1980) was a biologist who originally studied molluscs (publishing twenty scientific papers on them by the time he was 21), but moved into the study of the development of children's understanding, through observing them and talking and listening to them while they worked on exercises he set. His view of how children's minds work and develop has been enormously influential, particularly in educational theory. His particular insight was the role of maturation (simply growing up) in children's increasing capacity to understand their world; children cannot undertake certain tasks until they are psychologically mature enough to do so. His research spawned a great deal more study, much of which has undermined the detail of his own, but like many other investigators, his importance comes from his overall vision.

Piaget proposed that children's thinking does not develop entirely smoothly: instead, there are certain points at which it 'takes off' and moves into completely new areas and capabilities. He saw these transitions as taking place at about 18 months, 7 years and 11 or 12 years. This has been taken to mean that, before these ages, children are not capable (no matter how bright) of understanding things in certain ways, and has been used as the basis for scheduling the school curriculum (Atherton, 2002).[1] Piaget is a **cognitive theorist.** Piaget believed that the individual actively constructs knowledge about the world.

Piaget's Relevant Definitions[2]

Assimilation
The process by which a person takes material into their mind from the environment, which may mean changing the evidence of their senses to make it fit.

Accommodation
The difference made to one's mind or concepts by the process of assimilation. Note that assimilation and accommodation go together. You can't have one without the other.

Classification
The ability to group objects together on the basis of common features.

Class Inclusion
The understanding of more advanced than simple classification, that some classes or sets of objects are also sub-sets of a larger class. (e.g. there is a class of objects called dogs. There is also a class called animals. But all dogs are also animals, so the class of animals includes that of dogs).

Conservation
The realization that objects or sets of objects stay the same even when they are changed about or made to look different. For example, children can understand that the same amount of liquid is in two different shaped jars.

Developmental Norm
A statistical measure of typical scores for categories of information.

Egocentrism
The belief that you are the center of the universe and everything revolves around you: the corresponding inability to see the world as someone else does and adapt to it. Not moral "selfishness", just an early stage of psychological development. The move away from egocentrism is called decentration.

Elaboration
Relating new information to something familiar. An example would be learning how to cook a pasta dish. You may have cooked something similar in the past. In your mind your may think, "This is like that time I made Ramen except now I do…"

Operation
The process of working something out in your head. Young children (in the sensorimotor and pre-operational stages) have to act and try things out in the real world to work things out (like count on fingers). Older children and adults can do more in their heads.

Recognition
The ability to identify correctly something encountered before.

Recall
Being able to reproduce knowledge from memory.

Schema (or scheme)
The representation in the mind of a set of perceptions, ideas, and/or actions, which go together.

Stage
A period in a child's development in which he or she is capable of understanding some things but not others.

 Piaget's Stages of Development

This table was created by James Atherton and defines the different developmental stages according to Jean Piaget.[5]

Developmental Stage and Approximate Age	Characteristic Behavior
Sensory Motor Period **(0-24 months)**	
Reflexive Stage (0-2 months)	Simple reflex activity such as grasping and sucking.
Primary Circular Reactions (2-4 months)	Reflexive behaviors occur in stereotyped repetition such as opening and closing fingers repetitively.
Secondary Circular Reactions (4-8 months)	Repetition of actions to reproduce interesting consequences such as kicking one's feet to move a mobile suspended over the crib.
Coordination of Secondary Reactions (8-12 months)	Responses become coordinated into more complex sequences. Actions take on an "intentional" character such as the infant reaches behind a screen to obtain a hidden object.
Tertiary Circular Reactions (12-18 months)	Discovery of new ways to produce the same consequence or obtain the same goal such as the infant pulling a pillow toward him in an attempt to get a toy resting on it.
Invention of New Means Through Mental Combination (18-24 months)	Evidence of an internal representational system. Symbolizing the problem-solving sequence before actually responding. Deferred imitation.
The Preoperational Period **(2-7 years)**	
Preoperational Phase (2-4 years)	Increased use of verbal representation but speech is egocentric. The beginnings of symbolic rather than simple motor play. Transductive reasoning. Can think about something without the object being present by use of language.

Intuitive Phase (4-7 years)	Speech becomes more social, less egocentric. The child has an intuitive grasp of logical concepts in some areas. However, there is still a tendency to focus attention on one aspect of an object while ignoring others. Concepts formed are crude and irreversible. Easy to believe in magical increase, decrease, disappearance. Reality not firm. Perceptions dominate judgment. In the moral-ethical realm, the child is not able to show principles underlying best behavior. Rules of a game cannot develop in the mind; only uses simple do's and do not's imposed by authority.
Period of Concrete Operations (7-11 years)	
Evidence for organized, logical thought. There is the ability to perform multiple classification tasks, order objects in a logical sequence, and comprehend the principle of conservation. Thinking becomes less transductive and less egocentric. The child is capable of concrete problem solving. Some reversibility now possible (quantities moved can be restored such as in arithmetic: 3+4 = 7 and 7-4 = 3, etc.) Classifying logic-finding bases to sort unlike objects into logical groups where previously it was on superficial perceived attributes such as color. Categorical labels such as "number" or "animal" now available.	
Period of Formal Operations (11-15 years)	
Thought becomes more abstract, incorporating the principles of formal logic. The ability to generate abstract propositions, multiple hypotheses and their possible outcomes is evident. Thinking becomes less tied to concrete reality. Formal logical systems can be acquired. Can handle proportions, algebraic manipulation, and other purely abstract processes. If $a + b = x$ then $x = a - b$. If $ma/ca = IQ = 1.00$ then $Ma = CA$. Prepositional logic present, in as-if and if-then steps. Can use aids such as axioms to transcend human limits on comprehension. Can think hypothetically and test hypothesis. Based on the information in these stages, you can see it is important to have age appropriate materials in school.	

Piaget and Freud both agreed that environmental influences could affect the time spent in stages but not the order.

 Freud's Psychosexual Stages

Stage	Age	Description
Oral	Birth-1 Year	The new ego directs the baby's sucking activities toward breast or bottle. If oral needs are not met appropriately, the individual may develop such habits as thumb sucking, fingernail biting, pencil chewing, overeating and smoking.
Anal	1-3 Years	Young toddlers and preschoolers enjoy holding and releasing urine and feces. Toilet training becomes a major issue between parent and child. If parents insist that children be trained before they are ready or make too few demands, conflicts about anal control may appear in the form of extreme orderliness and cleanliness or messiness and disorder.
Phallic	3-6 Years	Id impulses transfer to the genitals, and the child finds pleasure in genital stimulation. Freud's Oedipus Conflict for boys and Electra Conflict for girls take place. Young children feel a sexual desire for the other-sex parent. To avoid punishment, they give up this desire and instead adopt the same-sex parent's characteristics and values. As a result, the superego is formed and children feel guilty each time they violate its standards. The relationships between id, ego and superego established at this time determine the individual's basic personality orientation.
Latency	6-11 years	Sexual instincts die down, and the superego develops further. The child acquires new social values from adults outside the family and from play with same-sex peers.
Genital	Adolescence	Puberty causes the sexual impulses of the phallic stage to reappear. If development has been successful during earlier stages, it leads to marriage, mature sexuality, and the birth and rearing of children.

Defense Mechanisms

Defense mechanisms are things that help us relieve stress. We can choose to accept, deny or change our perceptions and feelings to be in harmony with our values. Here is a list of the most common defense mechanisms and what they mean:

Denial
Complete rejection of the feeling or situation.

Suppression
Hiding the feelings and not acknowledging them.

Reaction Formation
Turning a feeling into the exact opposite feeling. For example, saying you hate someone you are interested in.

Projection
Projection is transferring your thoughts and feelings onto others. For example, someone who is being unfaithful themselves constantly accuses their partner of cheating.

Displacement
Feelings are redirected to someone else. Someone who has a bad day at work and can't complain goes home and yells at their kids instead.

Rationalization
You deny your feelings and come up with ways to justify your behavior.

Regression
Reverting to old behavior to avoid feelings.

Sublimation
A type of displacement, a redirection of the feeling into a socially productive activity.

 Maslow's Hierarchy of Needs

Maslow's Hierarchy of Needs consists of the following stages, from the top down:

- Self-actualization
- Esteem needs
- Belonging and love
- Safety
- Physical needs

These stages begin at physical needs. First you need to have food, water, and shelter before you can worry about other things. Once those needs are met, you may start to think of other things such as safety. You might buy a gun or move to a more prosperous and safe area. Once you are fed, clothed and safe, you will want to meet needs of belonging and love through relationships. If you feel loved, you may begin to think about your self-esteem and how you feel as a person, what you are contributing. The final stage, self-actualization, you may never meet. Most people do not.

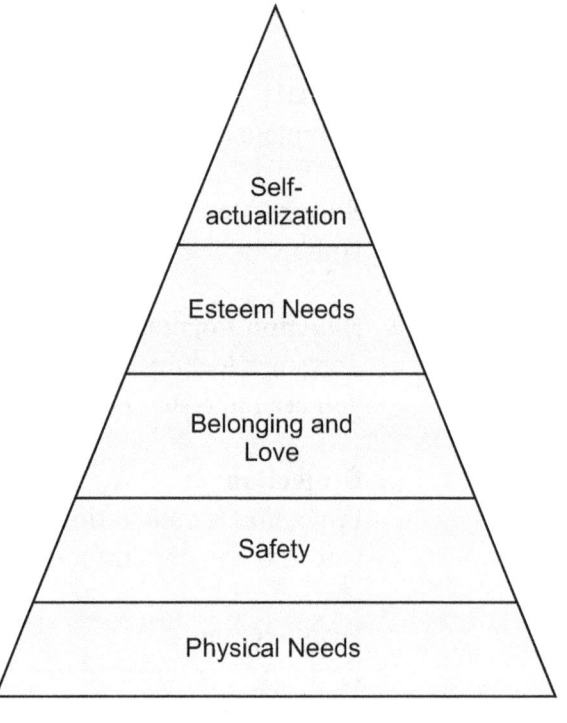

Maslow's Hierarchy of Needs

 Classical Conditioning

The first scientific experiment of classical conditioning was done by a Russian scientist named Ivan Pavlov. In Pavlov's famous dog experiment, he would ring a bell and then feed the dogs. Initially, the dogs would salivate when given food. Over time, the dogs began to salivate at the sound of the bell. Classical conditioning describes a link between a stimulus and a response in which a person or animal associates or substitutes a neutral stimulus, such as the bell, with the actual stimulus, the food. Many reflexive reactions, such as a person covering their eyes when something flies in front of their face, or salivating at the smell of their favorite food, can be explained through classical conditioning.

Operant Conditioning

Operant conditioning is a type of conditioning in which a person associates an action with a consequence. The main difference between operant conditioning and classical conditioning is that classical conditioning works more to explain reflexive or unconscious reactions, whereas operant conditioning works to explain elective actions and reactions. For example, a student will wish to do well in school because it brings the consequence of good grades and parental approval. Studies have shown that even infants can be taught certain behaviors using operant conditioning. The name most associated with operant conditioning is B. F. Skinner.

Reinforcers

Operant conditioning depends upon reinforcers as a method of learning. A reinforcer is anything which makes a behavior more likely to reoccur. Reinforcers can be positive or negative. A positive reinforcer is when something pleasant is used to make a behavior more likely. Parents paying their children for good grades or a person giving their pet a treat for doing a trick are both examples of positive reinforcers. A negative reinforcer is when something unpleasant is removed from a situation. For example, if a student studies more, they are less anxious. The anxiety is an unpleasant feeling which is removed as a result of studying, and therefore studying is a form of negative reinforcement. Conditioning can also occur using punishments, which instead of making a behavior more likely to reoccur, attempt to make it less likely to reoccur. Like reinforcers, punishments can be both positive and negative.

In addition to being positive and negative, reinforcers can also be described as extrinsic or intrinsic. An extrinsic reinforcer is something physical (tangible), or from the environment. Payment for work, a treat for doing well, and earning a prize for winning a game are all extrinsic reinforcers. An intrinsic reinforcer, on the other hand, is something which comes from within the individual, or in other words, something emotional. Self-satisfaction or the happiness which comes from praise are intrinsic reinforcers. The values of extrinsic and intrinsic reinforcers are different for everyone.

Behavior

Instructional conditioning gives a negative sanction. Extinction is done best gradually through shaping. **Extinction** is the process of unassociating the condition with the response. When you ring the bell for your cat to get dinner, then don't provide him with any food, gradually the cat will not come when the bell is sounded.

Response extinction is a method of modifying behavior. It ignores the behavior so you don't have the response.

Egocentric behavior means that a child does not take into consideration other people's needs. This is especially important in divorce situations where the child is in this stage. The child is incapable of understanding that they are not the result of the breakup because to that child, the world revolves around them.

Baby Albert was an experiment. There once was a boy who was kept in a box. Although it may sound fantastical, this was an actual experiment conducted. By using classical conditioning, the researchers made the baby afraid of rats.

Later, because of stimulus generalization, he was afraid of all furry animals. Most children's fears are learned through conditioning. This is a good example of unacceptable research ethics.

Stimulus generalization is when something from conditioning carries over to another related area. You are afraid of spiders; soon you become afraid of all bugs.

Social Learning Theory

The social learning theory combines the idea of conditioning, whether operant or classical, with the importance of environment and experience. A main focus of the social learning theory is modeling. The idea behind modeling is that people pattern their behavior off of others who they find admirable, or similar to themselves. Explicit role instruction (stereotypes), wherein boys play with trucks and cars, girls wear make-up.

Language Development

Language development begins at about six months. In all areas of the world and cultures, babies start cooing and babbling at six months. This is called pre-speech. The first element of development is the cooing. The second development is babbling. The third is hollow phrases. The fourth is telegraphic speech. Children in early language development are not able to understand figurative language, but they do understand some grammar. One example is the children's books where the main character is told to do a household chore. She is told to "run over these sheets with the iron" and she does just that, holds the iron in her hand and tramples the sheets. To learn more about language development, turn to suffix 1 to read additional information about the stages.

Echolalia is a baby repeating what you just said. At 10-14 months is when most children begin to speak actual words. A professor named Noam Chomsky stated that the ability to develop language skills is inherited in genes. Language theorists believe that a child acquires language through reinforcement from their environment. This would include all people they come in contact with and other things like television.

Telegraphic speech is a speech pattern in which a person eliminates function words from their sentences, instead keeping only the important content words. This is the sort of speech pattern which is typical for children around two years old. The sentences contain a noun and a verb in appropriate and logical order, however they aren't complete sentences. For example, a child would say "go home" instead of "I would like to go home now."

Fast Mapping

The term fast mapping was coined in 1978 by Susan Carey and Elsa Bartlett. Fast mapping is the process through which new words and concepts are learned after a single exposure. The theory explains how during the stage of language acquisition (when children are learning new words) children can understand the meaning and uses of a word after hearing them only once. Part of this occurs because they relate words they hear to ones they already know to determine the most probable meaning.

 Conducting Studies

Case Study
In a case study, a single individual (subject) is intensely studied. The researcher gets data through personal interviews with the subject, its employees, neighbors, contacts, etc., and by reviewing documentation or records (i.e., medical history, family life, etc.). Other sources for information are testing and direct observation of the subject. **Case studies used by Piaget and Freud led to wrong conclusions because they were not scientifically performed.**

Survey
A survey is a great way to get information about a specific type of information. For example, a survey would work well to measure performance in an office environment. These can be aggregated and used to improve employee performance. Usually with a survey, questionnaires are given out to participants who are then asked to answer questions to the best of their ability. When a participant fills out a survey themselves *about* themselves, it is called self-report data. This information can possibly not be as reliable as other research methods because subjects may be dishonest with their answers. For example, the question "Are you ever late to work?" may have respondents answering "no" when in fact, they are late but either do not remember that or are dishonest to avoid punishment or negative information about themselves. Many give the answers they feel that researchers (or themselves) want to hear instead of the truth.

Naturalistic Observation
Jean Piaget extensively used natural observation to study children. Naturalistic observation is when a researcher observes and studies subjects without interacting or interfering with them. Piaget observed the behavior of children playing in the schoolyard to assess developmental stages. Another example well known to television viewers of the series "Star Trek" involves "The Prime Directive". This is the most perfect version demonstrated (in fiction) of naturalistic observation. In the show, the researchers had the ability to view and study human cultures without being known to the subjects because of their advancements in technology. In the series, it was a great violation to interact with and impact the development of these cultures and societies.

Laboratory Observation
Laboratory observation is conducted in a laboratory environment. This method is selected to monitor specific biological changes in individuals. In a lab setting, expensive and sophisticated machinery can be used to study the participants. Sometimes one-way mirrors are used to observe the participants.

Psychological Tests

Psychological tests give information about participants. Some of the more common include standardized tests such as the Minnesota Multiphasic Personality Inventory also known as the MMPI (a personality test), aptitudes, interests, etc. A participant's score is then compared to the norms for that test. A test is valid if it measures what it is supposed to. For example, a test on depression will be able to measure a person's depression. If it cannot, then the test is not valid. Content validity is applied when a test measures something with more that one facet. For example, a test for overall cooking skills would not be valid if it only tested baking cakes and not other skills such as grilling meat or making soup.

Cross Sectional Studies

When people of different ages are studied at one particular time it is called a cross sectional study, because you have a cross section of the population or demographic that you want to study.

Longitudinal Studies

Longitudinal studies are when people are followed and studied over a long period of time and checked up on at certain points. These are best used to study the development of certain traits and track health issues. An example of a longitudinal study would be: 600 infants that were put up for adoption were tracked for several years. Some infants were adopted, some returned to the birth mothers and some were put into foster care. Which group adjusted the best and why? Lewis Terman did a longitudinal study of smart kids. The results are that the children are happy adults.

Correlation Research

Correlation research is used to show links between events, people, actions, behaviors, etc. Correlation research does not determine the causes of behavior but is linked to statistics. Causation is the cause of something. Correlation is not causation. This is an example of FAULTY, incorrect causation: a child eats an ice cream three times a week. This child scores well on school aptitude tests. It is determined that eating ice cream will make you smarter and do better on tests. There are additional factors or many others including socioeconomic status resulting from educated parents who genetically pass on their aptitude for school as well as their influence on the importance of school. In this situation, it is most likely the parents who contribute to the child's aptitude scores.

When conducting a survey and you have completed compiling the data, you will be able to measure the correlation between certain traits and variables tested. A correlation coefficient measures the strength between the two variables. A correlation coefficient is a number between -1 and +1.

A **positive correlation** means that when one variable increases, the other variable increases as well. For example, the more a couple fights, the more likely they are to get a divorce.

When one variable increases and the other variable decreases it is called a **negative correlation.** An example of this would be babies that are held by their caregivers tend to cry less. When the amount of time they are held goes up, the time they cry goes down.

The higher the number of the correlation coefficient, the stronger the correlation. A +0.9 or -0.9 shows a very strong correlation because the number is closest to a whole positive number 1 or a whole negative number 1. A weak correlation is a +0.1 or a -0.1. A correlation of zero shows that there is no relationship between variables.

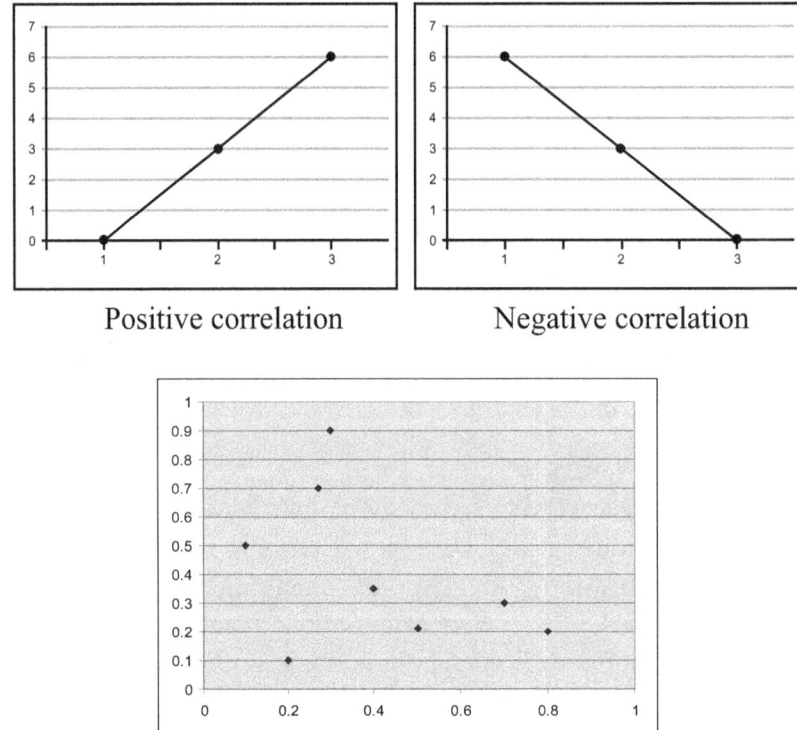

Positive correlation   Negative correlation

No correlation (above)

Census
A census is a collection of data from all cases or people in the chosen set. Usually, the most common form of a census would take place within an entire school or state. This means that every person of that school or state must be included. Censuses are usually not performed because they are so expensive. A census is valuable because it gives an accurate representation. To save time and money, survey companies will ask 1000 people or so (remember, the number changes based on the amount of people to be surveyed. A good rule of thumb is 10%). This is called sampling. For example, a recent

census shows that the single person is the fastest-growing household type. So basically, a sample is a set of cases of people randomly chosen from a large group. The sample is to represent the group. The larger the sample, the more accurate the results.

READING CHARTS AND GRAPHS

Charts and graphs are easy ways to display information and make it easily readable.

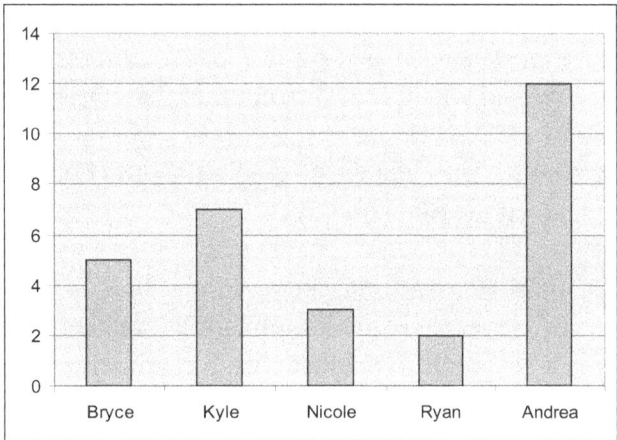

The above is a bar chart which shows five student's hours per week that they practice the piano. Are you able to tell who has the most hours and who has the least? How many hours per week does Nicole practice?

Name	Hours Per Week
Andrea	12
Bryce	5
Kyle	7
Nicole	3
Ryan	2

EXPERIMENTS

In experiments, a researcher manipulates variables to test theories and conclusions. Each experiment has independent and dependent variables. This is how researchers test cause and effect links and relationships.

The independent variable is the variable that researchers have direct control over. The dependent variable is then observed by the researcher.

In experiments, there are usually two groups of participants. One group is the experimental group and one group is the control group. The most common example is in medical trials. Let's say there is a trial run of a new diet drug. The researcher will split the group randomly in two. Group 1 will receive the diet pill that is being tested. Group 2 will receive a placebo pill. The placebo pill is simply a sugar pill. Group 2 will not know that they are not receiving the real drug. This allows the researchers to study the true effectiveness and side-effects of the pill. When the people are assigned to a group randomly, it is called **random assignment**. This particular experiment was a single-blind experiment. A **double-blind** experiment is when none of the doctors, researches and participants know who is getting the real drug. It is assigned by computer or an independent individual where it is kept confidential until the conclusion of the study.

When a participant starts to feel the effects of the drug but is *actually* taking a sugar pill or placebo it is called the **placebo effect**.

It is very important to avoid bias in research. Bias is the distortion of the results. Common types of bias include the sampling bias, subject bias and researcher bias. The placebo effect is an example of subject bias. Experimenter or researcher bias is avoided by conducting a double-blind experiment.

There are some disadvantages to experiments. They cannot be used to study everything. There are officially defined rules how humans and animals must be treated with the experiment. In an infamous experiment by psychologist Stanley Milgram, subjects were told that they were giving painful electric shocks to other people when in reality they were not. Some people consider this experiment unethical because it caused the participants emotional discomfort.

Researchers must get consent from their participants before conducting experiment. Informed consent means that the participants must know the content of the experiment and be warned of any risk or harm.

The **independent variable** in a study is the researchers have direct control over. Dependent variables are all other variables. The higher the correlation between the two factors is, the more closely the movement of one effects the movement of others.

Quantitative is a term used in research. It is used to describe something measurable, usually expressed as a number.

Qualitative is a term used to describe something similar in structure or organization.

Scientific Method is comprised of four steps:

1. Gather information

2. Generate hypothesis

3. Test hypothesis

4. Revise

Mean, median and mode are three important terms in analyzing and understanding data. The mean of a set of data is also called the average, because it is one method of determining the average or normal value for a set of data. To find an average, add all of the numbers in a data set and divide the total by the total number of data. For example the average of 3, 4, 5, and 6 is 3+4+5+6 which equals 28 divided by 4 because there are four numbers. 28/4= 4.5. Therefore, the average is 4.5.

The median is the middle number in a set of data. For example the median of the data set 3, 3, 4, 5, 6, 7, 8 is 5. The mode is the number which occurs the most often. For example, the mode of the data set 3, 3, 4, 5, 6, 6, 6, 7, 8, 9, 9 is 6 because it is the only number which occurs three times. All three are used together to give an accurate representation of the data.

Human Biology

Human development begins at fertilization.

Aspects of development are physical development, intellectual development, personality and social development.

Periods of life span:
- Prenatal stages (conception to birth)
- Infancy to toddlers (birth to 3 years)
- Early childhood (3-6 years)
- Middle childhood (6-12 years)
- Adolescence (12-20 years)
- Young Adulthood (20-40 years)
- Middle Adulthood (40-65 years)
- Late Adulthood (65+ years)

There are two different types of twins. **Monozygotic twins** are identical twins. **Dizygotic** twins are fraternal twins.

A gene is something that determines physical traits and is inherited from one or both parents.

A **zygote** is a fertilized ovum or egg.

Neonate is another name for newborn.

Prenatal development is a critical period, which is the first three months in the womb.

During the embryonic period, growth occurs in two directions. The first is **cephalocaudal**, or from the head downward. This means that the head develops faster than the rest of the body. The second type of growth is **proximodistal**, which is from the center (or spine) outward. This means that the vital organs begin to form before the extremities do.

Anoxia is a lack or deficiency of oxygen. This mostly happens during birth itself, by failing to breathe. Cerebral anoxia is more specifically a lack of oxygen to the brain. This can cause permanent damage and is a fairly common problem with infants. Anoxia is a problem in long labors, or if there are complications during birth. Additionally, infants born prematurely or with a very low birth weight have an increased risk of anoxia.

Body cells have 23 pairs. Men have 23 and women have 23 for a grand total of 46 chromosomes.

Down syndrome is caused by one extra chromosome, for a grand total of 47 chromosomes. To avoid this, parents need to conceive their children at younger ages. A woman's chance of having a Down syndrome baby at age 25 is 1 in 2500, at age 40 the odds are 1 in 100. Men over 55 also have a higher rate of fathering Down syndrome children. Down syndrome is where the child has one extra chromosome, which is number 21.

Mentally Retarded is defined as a low IQ and a mental age of about 4 years old. Of all health problems, those who are mentally retarded are the **least likely to have cerebral palsy as well.**

Autism is a lack of responsiveness to other people. Autism is rare in children of either sex in the first 2 ½ years. At birth, cells in the cerebral cortex are not well connected. They are lacking in myelin, which is insulation for nerves.

Rubella is a disease, also called German measles.

Critical period is a specific period in development when a certain event will have the greatest impact. For example, a certain species of bird has a certain period of time when their young can learn to fly. If they do not learn during that time, then they will never learn to fly.

Fetal alcohol syndrome is when babies have been in the womb when the mother was consuming alcohol. The problems include slowed growth, body and face malfunctions, nervous system disorders and mental retardation.

Fetal tobacco syndrome is what a baby can get if their mother smokes while pregnant. Five cigarettes are too many; the child will have problems, with a 50% greater risk of getting childhood cancer. The baby can also be born with a low birth weight.

Teratology is the study of substances which are harmful to prenatal development. These harmful substances are called **teratogens**. Teratogens are most harmful to the fetus and include alcohol, tobacco and other drugs including marijuana and cocaine. Diseases such as HIV, AIDS, and rubella are also teratogens, along with pollutants like mercury and radiation. Although the effects of teratogens are numerous and varied, it is nearly impossible to predict what effects will manifest when a teratogen has been present.

Amniocentesis is when a sample is taken from the fluid in the amnionic sac to be tested for various diseases or genetic traits.

For those giving birth, **medicated delivery** is the most popular. Dr. Grantly Dick Read started teaching natural prepared childbirth. **Gentle birth** is when the baby is born in a pool or bath with dim lights. **Cesarean birth** is a surgical delivery.

Ferdinand Lamaze taught women breathing procedures to get through childbirth. This includes panting.

Growth of the brain is not complete at birth. The cerebral cortex is the least developed part of a newborn.

 Development After Birth

Neonates have senses. This means that you can startle them in the womb with a loud noise. Their hearing is mostly developed. The eyes are not fully developed when babies are first born. They can distinguish color very early in their development. Newborns can track movement and bright objects.

Although many people believe that infants lack the ability to focus, this isn't true. The muscles involved in eye focus, called ciliary muscles, develop within about two months. After that, the real problem is with visual acuity the ability to see in detail. Visual acuity is determined by the brain's ability to process optical information and the development of the fovea, not the ability of the optical nerves. As the brain and fovea develop, an infant's eyesight develops.

Doctors agree that breast-feeding is the best way to feed your baby.

The "Virginia Apgar" sometimes referred to as the "Apgar Rating" is what doctors use to judge a baby when it is first born. It is rated on the following areas, getting a score of 0-2 in each area:

- Appearance
- Pulse
- Grimace (reflex, irritability)
- Activity
- Respiration

Infants have the capacity to learn. **Habituation**, a simple type of learning, is to get accustomed to something. Some people live near trains. When a train goes by your house every day, and in the night while you are asleep, it is easy to stop hearing the train. You become used to the noise and it does not bother you.

PKU is an enzyme deficiency. 1 in 14,000 will get it and will become mentally retarded if they do not receive treatment. They are tested in the first 3-6 weeks of life. PKU is short for **phenylketonuria.**

SIDS or Sudden Infant Death Syndrome is when there is an apnea, a temporary stoppage of breathing, which causes the baby to die.

The **Visual Cliff** shows that infants have depth perception. This is a study that was done by having infants placed on a solid, opaque surface. The infant's mothers were placed at the end of the table, where the opaque surface disappeared and glass began. The infants did not want to cross the glass because they could see the distance between where they were and the floor.

Temperament in infants is measured by monitoring:
- Irritability
- Social responsiveness
- Activity level

Object permanence is developed around age two. This means that a child will understand that once you leave the room, you are not gone forever. If you go around a corner, out of their vision, they know you are just around the corner.

According to the psychoanalytic theory, infants develop a secure attachment when a parent pays attention to, and responds appropriately to, the needs of the child. This is critical for the emotional development and security of a child.

John Bowlby's attachment theory states that infants need to form at least one strong attachment, such as to a parent, in order to develop normally. He also believed that the attachment held evolutionary purpose. The infant tends to want proximity to the person who cares for them as a form of self-preservation. According to Bowlby's theory, if a child feels that their caregiver is nearby and attentive, they feel confident to explore their surroundings. If not, they feel anxious and over time the become depressed.

Harry Harlow did an experiment with baby monkeys about affection and love. He took baby monkeys away from their mothers while they were still nursing and gave them two pretend monkeys in their cage. One was made of wire and had a bottle. The other was made of cloth but did not have a bottle. The monkeys preferred the one with cloth so much that they clung to it, only interacting with the wire monkey for food.

While it is not uncommon for young children to use different hands for different tasks, consistent hand preference, or hand dominance, begins to manifest between the ages of two and three and is cemented by age six. While being ambidextrous is often considered impressive or unique, it is generally recommended that children have a dominant hand to aid in learning fine motor skills and specialized activities. With cutting, for example, the dominant hand learns to use scissors, while the other hand learns to hold the paper effectively.

 Adolescence

Some theorists suggest that birth order helps determine the personality or behavioral traits of children. There are two basic stereotypes for the behavior of firstborn children, compliant and aggressive. In some cases firstborn children enjoy emulating or copying their parents in caring for and teaching younger siblings. They are cooperative, but they also crave approval. On the other end of the scale, some firstborn children are more aggressive. They are perfectionistic and motivated, but they also crave control. Firstborn children also tend to develop language skills faster than later born children because of the time they have one on one with their parents and the complete attention they receive during that time. They also tend to be more natural leaders and teachers.

The maturing of the body into an adult is done during puberty. This is done by the release of hormones that tell the body how to grow and respond. The pituitary gland is where these hormones are produced. One of the results of the hormones is the stimulation that matures the genitals.

During this time, girls begin menstruation. This is the body's way of preparing for future conception and procreation.

Because of hormones and the ways that each gender mature differently, there are some stereotypes that emerge. For example, boys are usually better in math, math reasoning, visual and spatial reasoning.

Typically mostly girls have difficulty with eating disorders. These can include **anorexia nervosa** which is self-starvation or **bulimia** which is a binging and purging (eat a lot then throw up so you don't gain weight).

Around this time, teenagers are beginning to complete their required schooling. However, for whatever reason, some do not complete it. Statistically, high school dropouts have almost a guarantee of poverty. Because of poverty and hunger, the school lunch system was started so that all children could get at least one "square" meal a day. Protein deficiency is generally found with lower class families. The majority of adolescents are similar to their parents in vocational values.

Another concern around this age are STDs. **STDs** are Sexually Transmitted Diseases which include AIDS and Herpes.

IQ Testing

There are many difficulties in measuring intelligence. Alfred Binet made the first IQ test. IQ tests are not a good indicator for children over a long period of time. It is possible to be coached in learning a particular type of question or test and have the score improve dramatically. IQ=Mental age divided by chronological age multiplied by 100.

$$IQ = MA/CA \times 100$$

IQ scores are only accurate for a short period of time. This measures a child against its peers.

Hyperactivity only affects **three percent** of all children. They have a short attention span.

Creative people are mostly **divergent** thinkers; this would include *gifted* or advanced children. **Divergent** thinking is a creative process. **Convergent** thinking is follower thinking.

Nature vs. Nurture is an old debate between two schools of thought. Nature means that a child will be born with whatever disposition, tastes and personality they were "meant" to have. Thos who believe in the nature theory think that there are bad seeds. Those who ascribe to the nurture view believe that all children are good, it is the way they are brought up that affects their personality and later, their actions.

Separated at birth, identical twins were studied and found later to have very similar jobs, haircuts, styles of dressing, etc. This shows that heredity has an impact. What does this study support? Nature or nurture? (Nature).

 Language Development

Language development begins at about six months. In all areas of the world and in the various cultures, babies start cooing and babbling at six months. This is called pre-speech. The first element of development is the cooing. The second development is babbling. The third is hollow phrases. The fourth is telegraphic speech. Children in early language development are not able to understand figurative language, but they do understand some grammar. One example is the children's book where the main character is told to do a household chore. She is told to "run over these sheets with the iron" and she does just that, holds the iron in her hand and tramples the sheets. To learn more about language development, turn to suffix 1 to read additional information about the stages.

Infants make various sounds, but around the age of six or seven months, these sounds begin including the repetition of meaningful sounds, such as "ma-ma" and "da-da." This stage of language development is described as babbling.

Along with the babbling comes gestures. During the period from 6 to 12 months old infants become increasingly proficient at making their wants clear through their gestures.

It is also interesting to note that children understand much of what is said to them, even before they are able to speak. For example, when asked "where's mommy?" a 10 month old will look in her direction. Most infants can also understand the word "no" long before they can talk.

Most children can speak a few, generally unclear, words by the age of one. By 18 months the vocabulary will expand to around 50 words. From here a child's vocabulary will begin to expand rapidly, reaching rates as high as 100 words a month. As infants are learning to speak, it is common for them to use holophrase speaking patterns combined with tone to get their meaning across. About six months after speaking their first words, children begin to string words together. All children learn at different rates, but the real indicator of proficiency is the ability to communicate, not the extent of vocabulary.

There are three main theories about language development. The first follows the idea of operant conditioning. Because babies are rewarded with attention or food when they say "mama" and "baba" they will continue to say those words and learn new ones. The other theory is that language abilities develop innately. This theory comes from Noam Chomsky, and states that since children all learn language rapidly, and around the same ages, there must be some mechanism in the brain which aids in language acquisition. Recent research has shown that language acquisition is likely just as much a result of either of these theories as it is of the social aspect of language. Children learn to speak from listening to their parents, especially through "baby talk," a term which describes not how infants sound, but how adults speak to infants. Infants learn early on to distinguish between the distinct sounds which are important to whichever language is spoken around them the most.

Echolalia is a baby repeating what you just said. At 10-14 months most children begin to speak actual words. Chomsky stated that the ability to develop language skills is inherited in genes. Language theorists believe that a child acquires language through reinforcement from their environment. This would include all people they come in contact with and other things like television.

The study of language is rather complex. The scientific study of words and sentences is called semantics. Opposites, synonyms, antonyms, and how sentences are put together are all subjects will fall under semantics. Holophrase syntax describes a communication style in which single words are used to communicate. This is typical of toddlers learning how to speak, for example "give" or "mama." The meaning is still understood, even though complete sentences are not used.

Morphemes are the smallest unit of a word which has meaning. Morphemes can be bound or free. A bound morpheme must be with a word. For example, in the word "impossible" the morpheme "im" is bound because it cannot be said alone. However, in the word "shipment" the morpheme ship is free because it can be a word on its own. Even smaller than morphemes, phonemes are also an area of study. Phonemes are the individual sounds. For example, in English there are 40 phonemes, created with different combinations of the 26 letters.

# *Id, Ego and Super Ego*

Sigmund Freud's analysis of human personality and the subconscious drives feature three main components: id, ego and superego. Together, these mechanisms combine to aide us in our decision-making and guide us to become the unique individuals that we all are. Robert Young, a professor in this area, provided the following information used to understand the id, superego and the ego:

<u>**The id**</u> contains the psychic content related to the primitive instincts of the body, notably sex and aggression, as well as all psychic material that is inherited and present at

birth. It functions entirely according to the pleasure-pain principle, its impulses either seeking immediate fulfillment or settling for a compromise fulfillment.

The superego is the ethical component of the personality and provides the moral standards by which the ego operates.

The ego coexists, in psychoanalytic theory with the id and superego. It is the integrator between the outer and inner worlds, as well as between the id and the superego. The ego gives continuity and consistency to behavior by providing a personal point of reference, which relates to the events of the past (retained in memory) and actions of the present and of the future (represented in anticipation and imagination). (SOURCE: Britannica.com.)

The main trio of Star Trek, the original TV series – McCoy, Kirk, and Spock – make for an interesting analogy of human personality as they each show characteristics of Freud's concepts of the id, ego, and superego. Hopefully, this analogy will make it easier for you to understand and remember this theory.

THE ID – James T. Kirk always enjoyed a good fight, risked his ship and crew often, and always fed his libido with an assortment of females. Kirk, with his passion for gratification in terms of aggression and sex, displays characteristics of the id.

THE SUPEREGO – Doctor Leonard (Bones) McCoy was always reminding his Captain of the rules and morality of any situation. He also is known for his arguments with Spock, just as the superego and ego are often in conflict.

THE EGO – Mr. Spock was the bringer of balance between the impulses of the id and the extreme caution of the superego by his use of logic and understanding of his Captain's needs as well as understanding the morality base of Bones. While Spock and Bones were often at odds, they always were working toward the same end – a correct and feasible solution to any given situation.

Together – Kirk, McCoy, and Spock represent the triadic conflict within all humans, thus three distinct characters, taken together to form an understanding of the human condition.[4]

Child Learning

Children learn to form their conscience to represent values communicated by their parents. Children watch their parents for cues for their actions and knowledge of what is acceptable behavior. Actions really do speak louder than words. The best way to teach children values is to do as one believes is correct.

Some children learn aggression through their peers. Think about that before you put your kids in daycare. Even children who learn to tolerate frustration can learn aggressive behavior.

Kibbutz

A Kibbutz is where a group of people live together and the children of all the people are raised by one or two people. The real parents of the children may see them for one hour a day. This is referred to as the hour of love. Think of modern day daycare. Children that are raised on the Kibbutz are used to study the effects of multiple caretakers. For example, they have more bland personality types because they have had to get along with their "new family." It is also difficult for them to create and maintain intimate relationships as they have a lack of emotional depth.

Kohlberg's Theory of Moral Development

Level 1: Preconventional morality

Stage 1: Punishment and obedience phase. Whether you will be punished or not determines what is moral or not. For example, you don't speed when driving the car because you know that you might get a ticket-a negative sanction from an authority figure.

Stage 2: A person becomes aware of two different viewpoints. You don't speed while driving a car because you want the lower rates on car insurance that you will get having no tickets on your record.

Level 2: Conventional morality

Stage 3: You do what is right in order to gain status or approval from other people or society. For example, you don't get speeding tickets while driving because in your circle of friends that would make you appear irresponsible, therefore lowering your social status.

Stage 4: A person abides by the law because they think that law is a higher order. It is their duty as a responsible citizen to not speed. This type of person would not run a red light in a deserted intersection even if he had been waiting five minutes. They believe that laws cannot be broken under any circumstance.

Level 3: Postconventional morality

Stage 5: A person is concerned with how their action might affect society, i.e., "I'm not going to speed because I might get into an accident and injure someone."

Stage 6: A person makes decisions according to his or her conscience. Not many, if any, people get to this stage.

Kohlberg believed that you went through stages one at a time and could not skip them. According to both Kohlberg and Piaget, the most immature reason to do something is to avoid punishment.

Childhood

Hurried child
For example, one that is always in a hurry, quick to eat, get ready, wash its face.

Resilient child
One that bounces back from a difficult situation like abuse.

Rite of passage
This is a signal to society that certain rules have changes. This person is no longer a child. Some examples of a rite of passage can include getting a drivers license, having sex for the first time, getting married, etc.

School phobia
Dread of school.

Childhood depression
Similar to adult depression usually exhibited as "nobody likes me."

The most direct measure of syntax in middle childhood is the mean link of the utterance (how long their sentences are).

Psychometrics
Cultural bias not generally known across all subcultures.

Mainstreaming
Putting disabled students with normal students. Children are most likely to achieve if their parents have set high standards and assist the children along the way. Gifted children often hide gifts to fit in.

Psychological maltreatment
Not physical abuse but when the child feels rejected or feels failure.

Self-concept
Who am I? Self-aware, recognized, defined.

Self-esteem
Begins in middle childhood.

Peer group
The other students in the environment where children live and attend school.

Stages of friendship:
0 Momentary playmates, ages 3-7
1 One way assistance, ages 4-9
2 Two way, fair weather, ages 6-12
3 Intimate, ages 9-15
4 Autonomous, interdependent, ages 12+

Behavior of a child with a difficult temperament can be managed by patient and consistent parenting. The amount of positive and helpful behavior of school-aged children correlates with the child's history of socialization. If someone wants to develop a secure attachment to a child, they must respond appropriately to their signals like picking up a baby when they cry. A father's role with an infant usually involves more play. Firstborn children are more likely to be motivated to achieve. Sibling rivalry is related to the ages of the children. Most children grow out of it.

Institutionalized Children
The negative effects of sensory deprivation (not as much attention) are more likely to increase with the length of the stage. Failure to thrive is caused by emotional neglect. They can look healthy but not be thriving. Children are easily stressed concerning divorce, moving and death.

Some health problems that children can get (duration ranging from 1 to 14 days) are measles, whooping cough, mumps, polio, and diphtheria. School exposure can help spread more epidemics and colds. Ninety-percent of all children in kindergarten are immunized.

Deferred imitation is the imitation of a past-observed behavior. A child may see their mother breastfeeding a sibling and may later copy the action with a doll.

Read to children to teach them to read. The Montessori method was created when teachers worked with mentally retarded kids. The teachers gave five-year-olds an Italian national exam and had success. The Montessori method teaches children to realize their full abilities.

Your identity changes as you are socialized (grow up). Family therapy involves the whole family. Some children have emotional disturbances while growing up, including bed-wetting, tics and stuttering. **Gender identity** is the awareness of being a male or female. **Gender conservation** is a child's realization their sex will stay the same.

There are different types of child play. They are in chronological order:

- Unoccupied behavior
- Onlooker
- Solitary independent (plays alone)
- Parallel play (plays around others but not with them)
- Associative
- Cooperative Play

Fear of the dark. For children about six years old, the fear is strong and can appear suddenly. This is what you should do:

- Accept the fear as normal
- Offer reassurance
- Encourage emotions freely

Parenting Styles

Authoritarian: "because I say so" – more prevalent in lower-class families.

Permissive: makes few demands, hardly ever punishes.

Authoritative: Respects individuality, but tries to instill social values.

Divorce

When children are in the preoperational stage, ages 3-6, they are egocentric and will, therefore, think every negative action is their fault. A male living with a single mom needs more affection. Girls living with single moms have difficulties with relationships with males in adolescence.

Benefits for Employed Mothers:

1. Mothers get confidence and satisfaction

2. Relieves financial pressure

3. Children are offered a wider variety of role models

Aging

Gerontology is the study of the aging process. Every moment we change, we age and grow a little older and hopefully, a little smarter. As our bodies change so do our lifestyle and our priorities. People who are working that experience discrimination because of their age, regardless if they are considered too old or too young, are victims of what is called ageism.

Most people experience at least some hearing loss by the age of 65. The loss of hearing that occurs with aging is termed presbycusis. Generally, presbycusis is believed to be a result of lifelong exposure to noise, although some theorize that the auditory functions in the brain decrease with age as well.

 *Sample Test Questions*

1) Which person believed that children were born a blank slate?

   A) Jean-Jacques Rousseau
   B) John Locke
   C) Alfred Binet
   D) Sigmund Freud
   E) Erik Erikson

The correct answer is B:) John Locke.

2) According to the social learning theory, behaviors and personalities develop as people

   A) Adjust their behavior to be less like people they dislike.
   B) Model themselves after people they admire or associate themselves with.
   C) Learn to get what they want through the process of trial and error.
   D) Repeatedly undergo the process of operant conditioning when developing their personalities.
   E) None of the above.

The correct answer is B:) Model themselves after people they admire or associate themselves with. Modeling is the central focus of the social learning theory.

3) Trust vs. Mistrust is Erikson's developmental stage which occurs while a

   A) Infant
   B) Toddler
   C) Preschooler
   D) School-age child
   E) Adolescent

The correct answer is A:) Infant.

4) _____ is the earliest sound a child makes to communicate.

   A) Babbling
   B) Cooing
   C) Echolalia
   D) Crying
   E) None of the above

The correct answer is D:) Crying.

5) A student is nervous about a test they have coming up so they decide to study an extra hour the night before. They can sleep well because they feel more prepared. The next day they take the test and feel confident about how they did. The test is returned to them and they have received a perfect score, and will get an A grade for the quarter. The student's parents are pleased and reward them by taking them out to dinner. Name all of the intrinsic reinforcers for the student in the story.

   A) Relieved anxiety, confidence, pleased parents
   B) Confidence, good grades, dinner
   C) Dinner, relieved anxiety, pleased parents
   D) Relieved anxiety, confidence
   E) Confidence, sleep well, pleased parents

The correct answer is D:) Relieved anxiety, confidence. This is the only answer which contains only intrinsic reinforcers, though all of the other answers do contain reinforcers. Pleased parents may seem like an intrinsic reinforcer, however the pleased feeling is for the parents, not the student, and the story does not actually indicate the student's response to their parent's approval.

6) _____ is the ethical component of personality and provides moral standards.

   A) Id
   B) Ego
   C) Superego
   D) Id and ego
   E) Superego and ego

The correct answer is C:) Superego.

7) The belief that you are the center of the universe

   A) Assimilation
   B) Accommodation
   C) Classification
   D) Conservation
   E) Egocentrism

The correct answer is E:) Egocentrism.

8) If a teacher rewards children with treats for participating in class, what type of conditioning is occurring?

   A) Positive reinforcing
   B) Negative reinforcing
   C) Positive punishment
   D) Negative punishment
   E) No conditioning is occurring

The correct answer is A:) Positive reinforcing. It is positive because the children are being given something they desire and it is reinforcement because the teacher wants to make them more likely to participate again.

9) A statistical measure of typical scores for categories of information

   A) Class inclusion
   B) Conservation
   C) Developmental norm
   D) Egocentrism
   E) Elaboration

The correct answer is C:) Developmental norm.

10) What was the visual cliff experiment designed to test?

   A) An infant's depth perception
   B) An infant's auditory capabilities
   C) An infant's visual acuity
   D) An infant's mental capabilities
   E) An infant's hand eye coordination

The correct answer is A:) An infant's depth perception. The visual cliff experiment was designed to see if an infant would crawl across a sheet of glass to their mother.

11) The first three weeks of prenatal growth are known as?

   A) Growing period
   B) Germinal period
   C) Fetus period
   D) Neonate period
   E) Embryo period

The correct answer is B:) Germinal period.

12) After a person moves to a new area they often hear airplanes flying overhead. After a week or two, they rarely notice them. What is this an example of?

   A) Auditory cliff
   B) Telegraphic speech
   C) Habituation
   D) Presbycusis
   E) Phoneme

The correct answer is C:) Habituation.

13) The process of being able to identify something encountered before

   A) Operation
   B) Recognition
   C) Recall
   D) Schema
   E) Stage

The correct answer is B:) Recognition.

14) Which of the following statements is the best example of telegraphic speech?

   A) My oldest and prettiest sister will visit with us next week
   B) My sister will visit next week
   C) Sister visit week
   D) My sister will be coming to visit me next week for three days
   E) None of the above

The correct answer is C:) Sister visit week. Telegraphic speech is a speech pattern which eliminates function words, and keeps only the content words of a sentence.

15) Which of the following correctly lists Freud's psychosexual stages in order?

   A) Latency, Oral, Phallic, Anal, Genital
   B) Anal, Oral, Latency, Phallic, Genital
   C) Genital, Latency, Oral, Phallic, Anal
   D) Phallic, Oral, Anal, Latency, Genital
   E) Oral, Anal, Phallic, Latency, Genital

The correct answer is E:) Oral, Anal, Phallic, Latency, Genital.

16) Generativity vs. Stagnation is Erikson's developmental stage which occurs while a(n)

   A) School-age child
   B) Adolescent
   C) Young adult
   D) Middle-age adult
   E) Old age

The correct answer is D:) Middle-age adult.

17) A set of perceptions, ideas or actions which go together

   A) Operation
   B) Recognition
   C) Recall
   D) Schema
   E) Stage

The correct answer is D:) Schema.

18) Which of the following does classical conditioning best explain?

   I. Reflexive reactions
   II. Unconscious actions
   III. Elective actions

   A) I only
   B) I and II only
   C) II and III only
   D) I, II and III
   E) I and III only

The correct answer is B:) I and II only. Classical conditioning explains reflexive and unconscious actions, but doesn't really explain elective actions, or things a person chooses to do.

19) According to Freud, at what age does the oral stage occur?

   A) Birth to 1 year old
   B) 1-3 years old
   C) 3-6 years old
   D) 6-11 years old
   E) Adolescence

The correct answer is A:) Birth to 1 year old.

20) Which parenting style is most likely to allow discussion about what the family vacation should be, without allowing the children to make the final decision?

   A) Authoritarian
   B) Authoritative
   C) Permissive
   D) Uninvolved
   E) All of the above are equally likely

The correct answer is B:) Authoritative. Authoritative parents use a rather democratic style, however still have expectations and rules, and they make the final decision.

21) Which of the following describes the theory of fast mapping?

   A) Children are able to learn new words and concepts after a single exposure to them.
   B) When a link is created between a stimulus and a response in which a person substitutes a neutral stimulus for the actual stimulus.
   C) When people pattern their behavior off of others who they find admirable, or similar to themselves.
   D) An infant needs to form at least one strong attachment in order to develop normally.
   E) None of the above.

The correct answer is A:) Children are able to learn new words and concepts after a single exposure to them. Answer B describes classical conditioning, answer C describes modeling, and answer D describes the attachment theory.

22) Which of the following statements is TRUE?

   A) Parents should encourage their children to become ambidextrous because it will make them more efficient in performing tasks which require fine motor skills.
   B) Parents should encourage their children to use their right hand because right handed children tend to be better readers than left handed children.
   C) Parents should encourage their children to use their left hand because this stimulates right brain growth.
   D) It doesn't matter if children are right or left handed. However, it is encouraged that they are one or the other, to aid in the development of fine motor skills.
   E) None of the above statements are true.

The correct answer is D:) It doesn't matter if children are right or left handed. However, it is encouraged that they are one or the other, to aid in the development of fine motor skills.

23) Which is the second stage of Maslow's Hierarchy of Needs?

   A) Self-actualization
   B) Esteem needs
   C) Belonging and love
   D) Safety
   E) Physical needs

The correct answer is D:) Safety.

24) Determine the mode and mean of the following set of numbers respectively:

23, 24, 27, 25, 26, 24, 28, 3, 6, 1

A) 24.5, 18.7
B) 24, 18.7
C) 24, 24.5
D) 25, 24.5
E) 18.7, 24

The correct answer is B:) 24, 18.7. The mean is 18.7, and the mode is 24 because it occurs twice and the other numbers occur only once.

25) Which defense mechanism occurs when someone hides their feelings and does not acknowledge them?

A) Denial
B) Suppression
C) Reaction formation
D) Projection
E) Displacement

The correct answer is B:) Suppression.

26) At what age does language expand rapidly in children?

A) 12 months
B) 18 months
C) 2 years
D) 3 years
E) 5 years

The correct answer is B:) 18 months. This is just after they hit the 50 word milestone and language acquisition can reach rates as high as 100 words a month.

27) Which of the following statements is TRUE?

   A) Firstborn children are always aggressive. They are perfectionists and crave control.
   B) Firstborn children follow no stereotypes whatsoever and do not differ in any meaningful ways from later born children.
   C) Firstborn children are always compliant. They follow their parent's examples and become cooperative and nurturing towards younger siblings.
   D) Although not all firstborn children follow the same stereotypes, they tend to fall into two distinct behavioral groups.
   E) All of the above are incorrect.

The correct answer is D:) Although not all firstborn children follow the same stereotype, they tend to fall into two distinct behavioral groups. Compliant and aggressive stereotypes are described in A and C.

28) What type of research is conducted by watching the subject?

   A) Naturalistic observation
   B) Longitudinal research
   C) Conditioning
   D) Operant conditioning
   E) Extinction

The correct answer is A:) Naturalistic observation.

29) According to Freud, a child being potty trained is in which stage of psychosexual development?

   A) Phallic
   B) Genital
   C) Latency
   D) Anal
   E) Oral

The correct answer is D:) Anal.

30) Which defense mechanism occurs when someone turns a feeling into the exact opposite feeling?

  A) Denial
  B) Suppression
  C) Reaction formation
  D) Projection
  E) Displacement

The correct answer is C:) Reaction formation.

31) Which of the following is most directly harmed by teratogens?

  A) Zygote
  B) Embryo
  C) Fetus
  D) Zygote and Embryo
  E) Embryo and Fetus

The correct answer is C:) Fetus. Teratogens are harmful agents which can cause birth defects and are harmful to the fetus.

32) If a parent grounds a child from the computer after they fail a test, which of the following best describes the type of conditioning?

  A) Positive reinforcing
  B) Negative reinforcing
  C) Positive punishment
  D) Negative punishment
  E) No conditioning is occurring

The correct answer is D:) Negative punishment. It is negative because a privilege was taken away.

33) Identity vs. Role Confusion is Erikson's developmental stage which occurs while a

  A) Infant
  B) Toddler
  C) Preschooler
  D) School-age child
  E) Adolescent

The correct answer is E:) Adolescent.

34) Which defense mechanism occurs when someone redirects stress into a socially productive activity?

   A) Rationalization
   B) Regression
   C) Sublimation
   D) Projection
   E) Displacement

The correct answer is C:) Sublimation.

35) Which of the following best characterizes the Preconventional stage of moral development?

   I. Self interest and punishment orientation
   II. Interpersonal accord orientation
   III. Universal ethical principles orientation

   A) I and II only
   B) I only
   C) I and III only
   D) II and III only
   E) I, II and III

The correct answer is B:) I only. The Preconventional stage is characterized by self-interest and punishment orientation.

36) Initiative vs. Guilt is Erikson's developmental stage which occurs while a

   A) Infant
   B) Toddler
   C) Preschooler
   D) School-age child
   E) Adolescent

The correct answer is C:) Preschooler.

37) Which of the following are NOT extrinsic reinforcers?

   A) Money
   B) Satisfaction
   C) Prizes
   D) Food
   E) All of the above are extrinsic reinforcers

The correct answer is B:) Satisfaction. Money, prizes and food are all extrinsic reinforcers because they are tangible. Satisfaction, however, is intrinsic because it is emotional and intangible.

38) Which is the fourth stage of Maslow's Hierarchy of Needs?

   A) Self-actualization
   B) Esteem needs
   C) Belonging and love
   D) Safety
   E) Physical needs

The correct answer is B:) Esteem needs.

39) Which of the following is an example of Maslow's first level of needs?

   A) Food
   B) School
   C) Car
   D) Travel
   E) Church

The correct answer is A:) Food.

40) Which of the following correctly lists the levels of Maslow's hierarchy of needs from lowest to highest?

   A) Safety, esteem, physiological, love and belonging, self-actualization
   B) Self-actualization, esteem, safety, love and belonging, physiological
   C) Physiological, esteem, love and belonging, self-actualization, safety
   D) Safety, physiological, love and belonging, esteem, self-actualization
   E) Physiological, safety, love and belonging, esteem, self-actualization

The correct answer is E:) Physiological, safety, love and belonging, esteem, self-actualization. Answer D is the second closest answer, however it swaps the first two levels.

41) The ability to group objects together on the basis of common features

   A) Assimilation
   B) Accommodation
   C) Classification
   D) Conservation
   E) Egocentrism

The correct answer is C:) Classification.

42) According to Freud, at what age does the phallic stage occur?

   A) Birth to 1 year old
   B) 1-3 years old
   C) 3-6 years old
   D) 6-11 years old
   E) Adolescence

The correct answer is C:) 3-6 years old.

43) Which stage of moral development is characterized by adherence to universal ethical principles?

   A) Preconventional
   B) Preconventional or conventional
   C) Postconventional
   D) Conventional
   E) Any of the above could be correct without more information

The correct answer is C:) Postconventional. The Postconventional stage of moral development is the final stage, and it is characterized by conscience and adherence to ethical principles.

44) Which of the following is an example of Maslow's third level of needs?

   A) Sex
   B) Money
   C) Love
   D) Transportation
   E) Home

The correct answer is C:) Love.

45) _____ is when a variable from conditioning carries over to another related area.

- A) Stimulus generalization
- B) Longitudinal research
- C) Conditioning
- D) Operant conditioning
- E) Extinction

The correct answer is A:) Stimulus generalization.

46) Which of the following BEST describes self-actualization?

- A) To overcome loneliness and alienation, and to receive and give love.
- B) The need to understand and fulfill one's purpose or desire in life.
- C) The basic biological needs such as water, oxygen, and food.
- D) To have self esteem and to receive praise and approval from others.
- E) The need to have a safe and secure environment.

The correct answer is B:) The need to understand and fulfill one's purpose or desire in life.

47) Ritalin is a well-known drug used to treat

- A) Habituation
- B) Object permanence
- C) Hyperactivity
- D) Divergence
- E) Convergence

The correct answer is C:) Hyperactivity.

48) When a baby repeats things that it has heard it is called

- A) Baby talk
- B) Echolalia
- C) Phonetic speech
- D) Speech pattern
- E) None of the above.

The correct answer is B:) Echolalia.

49) According to Maslow's theory, which of the following is TRUE?

   A) A person must feel safe to be concerned about hunger.
   B) A person must feel loved to feel safe and secure.
   C) A person must feel safe to have self-esteem.
   D) A person must achieve self-actualization to have self-esteem.
   E) A person must achieve self-actualization before they feel safe.

The correct answer is C:) A person must feel safe to have self-esteem. Esteem is higher up in Maslow's hierarchy of needs than is safety. They other options all have the order wrong.

50) Which of the following statements is NOT true?

   A) In operant conditioning, a person associates an action with a consequence.
   B) B. F. Skinner the person most associated with operant conditioning.
   C) Studies have shown that operant conditioning requires extensive neural development, and therefore cannot be applied until a subject is at least twelve years of age.
   D) Operant conditioning best explains elective actions.
   E) None of the above.

The correct answer is C:) Studies have shown that operant conditioning requires extensive neural development, and therefore cannot be applied until a subject is at least twelve years of age. Studies have actually shown that operant conditioning can be used to even teach infants, although the processes do become more complex the older a person gets.

51) When something is measurable in number it is

   A) Naturalistic observation
   B) Qualitative
   C) Cross sectional studies
   D) Quantitative
   E) Extinction

The correct answer is D:) Quantitative.

52) Which of the following represents that strongest correlation?

   A) -.10
   B) +.23
   C) -.44
   D) +.89
   E) +.55

The correct answer is D:) +.89.

53) Which is NOT a step in the scientific method?

   A) Gather information
   B) Generate hypothesis
   C) Test hypothesis
   D) Revise
   E) None of the above.

The correct answer is E:) None of the above.

54) Which defense mechanism occurs when someone redirects their feelings, positive or negative, towards someone else?

   A) Denial
   B) Suppression
   C) Reaction formation
   D) Projection
   E) Displacement

The correct answer is D:) Projection.

55) Which of the following is NOT one of Erikson's eight stages of development?

   A) Trust vs. Mistrust
   B) Initiative vs. Guilt
   C) Autonomy vs. Doubt and Shame
   D) Identity Role vs. Role Confusion
   E) Intimacy vs. Stagnation

The correct answer is E:) Intimacy vs. Stagnation.

56) Dr. Smith studied a brother and sister for three years. This represents

   A) Longitudinal research
   B) Cross sectional studies
   C) Naturalistic observation
   D) An experiment
   E) A case study

The correct answer is E:) A case study.

57) The process by which a person takes material into their mind from the environment is

   A) Assimilation
   B) Accommodation
   C) Classification
   D) Conservation
   E) Egocentrism

The correct answer is A:) Assimilation.

58) Which system is vulnerable for the most time after conception?

   A) Reproductive system
   B) Central nervous system
   C) Glandular system
   D) Digestive system
   E) Sensory system

The correct answer is B:) Central nervous system.

59) An infant will look at an object that he prefers for _____ than an object he has no interest in.

   A) A longer time
   B) A shorter time
   C) The same amount of time
   D) 30 seconds shorter
   E) None of the above.

The correct answer is A:) A longer time.

60) According to Freud, at what age does the genital stage occur?

   A) Birth to 1 year old
   B) 1-3 years old
   C) 3-6 years old
   D) 6-11 years old
   E) Adolescence

The correct answer is E:) Adolescence.

61) According to Erikson, what is the first stage of development?

   A) Trust vs. Mistrust
   B) Identity Role vs. Role Confusion
   C) Generativity vs. Stagnation
   D) Initiative vs. Guilt
   E) Autonomy vs. Doubt and shame

The correct answer is A:) Trust vs. Mistrust. This stage lasts from infancy to around 18 months.

62) When an infant no longer responds to a new toy he is showing

   A) Habituation
   B) Object permanence
   C) Hyperactivity
   D) Divergence
   E) Convergence

The correct answer is A:) Habituation.

63) An infant startling at a noise is what type of reflex?

   A) Simple
   B) Beginning
   C) First level
   D) Second level
   E) Intermediate

The correct answer is A:) Simple.

64) _____ theories are based on the idea that our actions are deeply influenced by our unconscious.

   A) Humanistic
   B) Psychoanalytical
   C) Cognitive
   D) Learning
   E) None of the above.

The correct answer is B:) Psychoanalytical.

65) _____ theorists are concerned with the effects of various types of conditioning.

   A) Humanistic
   B) Psychoanalytical
   C) Cognitive
   D) Learning
   E) None of the above.

The correct answer is D:) Learning.

66) According to Erikson's stages of development, toddler's exploring their environment's are in which stage?

   A) Trust vs. Mistrust
   B) Autonomy vs. Shame and Doubt
   C) Initiative vs. Guilt
   D) Industry vs. Inferiority
   E) Identity vs. Role Confusion

The correct answer is B:) Autonomy vs. Shame and Doubt. As a toddler explores their environment and learns their limitations and abilities they are in the stage of conflict between autonomy versus shame and doubt.

67) Which of the following is a humanist?

   A) Maslow
   B) Freud
   C) Piaget
   D) Apgar
   E) Erikson

The correct answer is A:) Maslow.

68) From week eight until conception is known as?

   A) Growing period
   B) Germinal period
   C) Fetus period
   D) Neonate period
   E) Embryo period

The correct answer is C:) Fetus period.

69) The amount of words spoken in a sentence is linked to

   A) Mean length of utterance
   B) Echolalia
   C) Telegraphic speech
   D) Cooing
   E) Babbling

The correct answer is A:) Mean length of utterance.

70) According to Freud's personality theory, which of the following is present at birth?

   A) Id
   B) Ego
   C) Superego
   D) Id and ego
   E) Superego and ego

The correct answer is A:) Id.

71) Which of the following describes growth from the head downward?

   A) Acuital
   B) Cephalocaudal
   C) Proximodistal
   D) Presbycusis
   E) Hierarchical

The correct answer is B:) Cephalocaudal. This basically means that the head develops faster than the rest of the body.

72) Social smile appears at how many weeks?

   A) 2
   B) 4
   C) 7
   D) 9
   E) 13

The correct answer is C:) 7.

73) Which of the following correctly lists Piaget's four stages of cognitive development?

   A) Sensorimotor, Preoperational, Formal Operational, Concrete Operational
   B) Concrete Operational, Sensorimotor, Preoperational, Formal Operational
   C) Preoperational, Sensorimotor, Concrete Operational, Formal Operational
   D) Sensorimotor, Preoperational, Concrete Operational, Formal Operational
   E) Formal Operational, Concrete Operational, Preoperational, Sensorimotor

The correct answer is D:) Sensorimotor, Preoperational, Concrete Operational, Formal Operational.

74) Aggression in 4 and 5 year olds is usually _____ related.

   A) People
   B) Possession
   C) Food
   D) Sleep
   E) Attention

The correct answer is B:) Possession.

75) A parent who makes few demands on a child shows what parenting style?

   A) Permissive
   B) Authoritative
   C) Authoritarian
   D) Indulgent
   E) Spoiling

The correct answer is A:) Permissive.

76) According to Piaget's theory, if a child uses a carrot as a gun during symbolic play, they are

   A) Angry, and using it to get out their aggression.
   B) Learning through the use of symbolic play.
   C) Undergoing a stage where they learn to be independent.
   D) Working to fulfill the basic need of safety.
   E) None of the above.

The correct answer is B:) Learning through the use of symbolic play. In the preoperational stage of cognitive development, children use symbolic thinking to understand the world.

77) According to John Bowlby's attachment theory, if a child feels their caregiver is nearby and attentive

   A) They feel confident to explore their surroundings.
   B) It will not affect their behavior in any way.
   C) They feel stifled and will become depressed.
   D) They will fail to develop normally because they will always feel pressured.
   E) None of the above.

The correct answer is A:) They feel confident to explore their surroundings. The attachment theory states that infants need to form at least one meaningful attachment to develop normally, and feel confident.

78) The effects of regularly watching of the television program Sesame Street are positive only among

   A) Black children
   B) White children
   C) Lower income children
   D) No difference in race or economic status
   E) None of the above.

The correct answer is D:) No difference in race or economic status.

79) Which of the following terms describes the gradual loss of hearing which occurs with aging?

   A) Presbycusis
   B) Promimodistal hearing loss
   C) Natural hearing loss
   D) Holophrase hearing loss
   E) None of the above.

The correct answer is A:) Presbycusis. Presbycusis is believed to be the result of life-long exposure to noise.

80) Who is most associated with the idea of operant conditioning?

   A) Ivan Pavlov
   B) Susan Carey
   C) Sigmund Freud
   D) Madame Marie Curie
   E) B. F. Skinner

The correct answer is E:) B. F. Skinner.

81) When someone assumes they will fail and do not even try to complete a task this is called

   A) Learned helplessness
   B) Negative effect
   C) Consequence
   D) Failure
   E) Classical conditioning

The correct answer is A:) Learned helplessness.

82) When is anoxia most likely to be a problem for infants?

   A) First trimester
   B) Second trimester
   C) Third trimester
   D) During birth
   E) Between one and two months old

The correct answer is D:) During birth. Anoxia becomes a risk during long labor or if complications occur.

83) A parent who ignores a child's temper tantrum is hoping to discourage future tantrums by

- A) Positive reinforcement
- B) Negative reinforcement
- C) Modeling
- D) Extinction
- E) Classical conditioning

The correct answer is D:) Extinction.

84) According to Piaget's theory of cognitive development, in what stage can a person comprehend abstract thought?

- A) Formal operational
- B) Concrete operational
- C) Sensorimotor
- D) Preoperational
- E) All of the above

The correct answer is A:) Formal operational. This is the final stage of cognitive development, ranging from around age 12 into adulthood.

85) Who coined the term modeling?

- A) Freud
- B) Piaget
- C) Bandura
- D) Erikson
- E) Kohlberg

The correct answer is C:) Bandura.

86) Which of the following terms describes growth from the spine outward?

- A) Acuital
- B) Cephalocaudal
- C) Proximodistal
- D) Presbycusal
- E) Hierarchical

The correct answer is C:) Proximodistal. This means that the vital organs begin developing before the extremities do.

87) About how long does it take to develop the muscles necessary for the eye to focus?

    A) 2 days
    B) 2 weeks
    C) 2 months
    D) 2 years
    E) The amount is so varied that it cannot be estimated

The correct answer is C:) 2 months. After two months, infant's vision is still blurry because the fovea and brain aren't developed enough to process optical information.

88) At what age does hand preference begin to manifest?

    A) 6-8 months
    B) 1-2 years
    C) 2-3 years
    D) 3-5 years
    E) 6 years

The correct answer is C:) 2-3 years. If hand preference begins to develop long before this, it may be a sign that one hand doesn't function well.

89) Which of the following best describes the morphemes in the word "unbreakable"?

    A) 1 bound morpheme and 2 free morphemes
    B) 2 bound morphemes and 1 free morpheme
    C) 3 bound morphemes and no free morphemes
    D) No bound morphemes and 3 free morphemes
    E) There are 6 distinct morphemes in the word

The correct answer is A:) 1 bound morphemes and 2 free morphemes. The morphemes are "un," "break" and "able." "Un" is bound, and "break" and "able" are free.

90) Which of the following statements is NOT true?

   A) Most children can speak a few words by the time they are 12 months old.
   B) One theory of language development is that infants undergo repeated operant conditioning.
   C) Children learn to understand words at the same time they learn to speak them.
   D) Infants learn early on to distinguish between distinct sounds.
   E) None of the above.

The correct answer is C:) Children learn to understand words at the same time they learn to speak them. Infants and children often comprehend words long before they are able to communicate themselves. An example of this is the word "no."

91) Which of the following theories was developed by Susan Carey?

   A) Theory of cognitive development
   B) Social learning theory
   C) Fast mapping
   D) Proximodistal development
   E) Hierarchy of needs

The correct answer is C:) Fast mapping. The theory of fast mapping was developed by Susan Carey and Elsa Bartlett in 1978.

92) Who is most associated with the idea of classical conditioning?

   A) Ivan Pavlov
   B) B. F. Skinner
   C) Susan Carey
   D) Sigmund Freud
   E) None of the above.

The correct answer is A:) Ivan Pavlov. Pavlov is famous for his experiment with bells and dogs.

93) Which of the following is the main focus of the social learning theory?

   A) Learning through operant conditioning exclusively
   B) Learning through classical conditioning exclusively
   C) Learning through operant and classical conditioning
   D) Learning and development through the process of modeling
   E) None of the above.

The correct answer is D:) Learning and development through the process of modeling. Modeling is the central focus of social learning theory.

94) According to Freud, a child who hasn't reached puberty and who mostly plays with friends of the same gender is in which stage of psychosexual development?

   A) Phallic
   B) Genital
   C) Latency
   D) Anal
   E) Oral

The correct answer is C:) Latency.

95) Which of the following correctly orders Kohlberg's three levels of moral development?

   A) Preconventional, conventional, postconventional
   B) Preconventional, postconventional, conventional
   C) Conventional, preconventional, postconventional
   D) Conventional, postconventional, preconventional
   E) Postconventional, conventional, postconventional

The correct answer is A:) Preconventional, conventional, postconventional.

96) Which of the following have the highest risk of anoxia?

   A) Infants born more than two weeks late
   B) Infants born prematurely
   C) Infants with a relatively high birth weight
   D) Children between the ages of three and five
   E) Children between the ages of one and two

The correct answer is B:) Infants born prematurely. This is in part because infants born prematurely generally have a very low birth weight which is a risk factor of anoxia.

97) Which of the following best describes the attachment theory?

    A) Attachment to a parent is essential to development in infants.
    B) An infant's desire for proximity to the person who cares for them is a form of self-preservation.
    C) A child who forms no attachments is more likely to form attachments later in life.
    D) If an infant is separated from their main caregiver for an extended time they will become depressed.
    E) A, B and D all correctly describe the attachment theory.

The correct answer is E:) A, B and D all correctly describe the attachment theory. The attachment theory was developed by John Bowlby. Answer C is not a part of the attachment theory.

98) Which of the following are involved in determining visual acuity?

    I. Brain
    II. Fovea
    III. Ciliary muscles

    A) I only
    B) II only
    C) II and III only
    D) I and II only
    E) I, II and III

The correct answer is D:) I and II only. The brain and fovea determine visual acuity, whereas the ciliary muscles are involved in focusing the eye's lens.

99) Determine the mean and median of the following set of numbers respectively

    2, 4, 7, 23, 27, 28, 4, 26

    A) 15.1, 15
    B) 15.1, 23
    C) 23, 15.1
    D) 18.5, 15.1
    E) 15.1, 18.5

The correct answer is A:) 15.1, 15. The median is 15 because there is an even amount of numbers. When this happens, the two middle numbers are averaged together. In this case $(7+23)/2 = 15$.

100) Which of the following is NOT a general characteristic of firstborn children?

   A) Develop language skills faster
   B) Natural leaders
   C) Troublemakers
   D) Natural teachers
   E) All of the above are characteristics of firstborn children

The correct answer is C:) Troublemakers. A, B, and D are all generally characters of firstborn children.

101) What is the term which describes a toddler who communicates in single word phrases such as "baba"?

   A) Semantic
   B) Phoneme
   C) Morpheme
   D) Presbycusis
   E) Holophrase syntax

The correct answer is E:) Holophrase syntax. Holophrase syntax describes single word communication.

102) Which of the following is a teratogen?

   A) Alcohol
   B) Tobacco
   C) HIV
   D) Radiation
   E) All of the above

The correct answer is E:) All of the above. Exposure to teratogens can cause many different and rather unpredictable side effects in unborn children.

 *Test-Taking Strategies*

Here are some test-taking strategies that are specific to this test and to other CLEP tests in general:
- Keep your eyes on the time. Pay attention to how much time you have left.
- Read the entire question and read all the answers. Many questions are not as hard to answer as they may seem. Sometimes, a difficult sounding question really only is asking you how to read an accompanying chart. Chart and graph questions are on most CLEP tests and should be an easy free point.
- If you don't know the answer immediately, the new computer-based testing lets you mark questions and come back to them later if you have time.
- Read the wording carefully. Some words can give you hints to the right answer. There are no exceptions to an answer when there are words in the question such as always, all or none. If one of the answer choices includes most or some of the right answers, but not all, then that is not the answer. Here is an example:

   The primary colors include all of the following:
   A) Red, Yellow, Blue, Green
   B) Red, Green, Yellow
   C) Red, Orange, Yellow
   D) Red, Yellow, Blue
   E) None of the above.

   Although item A includes all the right answers, it also includes an incorrect answer, making it incorrect. If you didn't read it carefully, were in a hurry, or didn't know the material well, you might fall for this.
- Make a guess on a question that you do not know the answer to. There is no penalty for an incorrect answer. Eliminate the answer choices that you know are incorrect. For example, this will let your guess be a 1 in 3 chance instead.

 *What Your Score Means*

Based on your score, you may, or may not, qualify for credit at your specific institution. At University of Phoenix, a score of 50 is passing for full credit. At Utah Valley State College, the score is unpublished, the school will accept credit on a case-by-case basis. Another school, Brigham Young University (BYU) does not accept CLEP credit. To find out what score you need for credit, you need to get that information from your school's website or academic advisor.

You can score between 20 and 80 on any CLEP test. Some exams include percentile ranks. Each correct answer is worth one point. You lose no points for unanswered or incorrect questions.

 Test Preparation

How much you need to study depends on your knowledge of a subject area. If you are interested in literature, took it in school, or enjoy reading then your studying and preparation for the literature or humanities test will not need to be as intensive as someone who is new to literature.

This book is much different than the regular CLEP study guides. This book actually teaches you the information that you need to know to pass the test. If you are particularly interested in an area, or you want more information, do a quick search online. There is a lot you'll need to memorize. Almost everything in this book will be on the test. It is important to understand all major theories and concepts listed in the table of contents. It is also very important to know any bolded words.

Don't worry if you do not understand or know a lot about the area. With minimal study, you can complete and pass the test.

One of the fallacies of other test books is test questions. People assume that the **content** of the questions are similar to what will be on the test. **That is not the case.** They are only to test your "test taking skills" so for those who know to read a question carefully, there is not much added value from taking a "fake" test.

To prepare for the test, make a series of goals. Allot a certain amount of time to review the information you have already studied and to learn additional material. Take notes as you study-it will help you learn the material.

 **Suffix 1**

Language Development in the Early Years Prepared by: Mei-Yu Lu

ERIC Clearinghouse on Reading, English, and Communication Digest #154

The Social Root of Language Development

This digest, written from a social interaction perspective, provides readers an overview of children's language development in the first five years of their life. The primary function of language, according to Vygotsky (1962), "in both adults and children is communication, social contact" (p.19). Through daily interaction with other language users, children learn how to use language to convey messages, to express feelings, and to achieve intentions which enable them to function in a society. Muspratt, Luke, and Freebody (1997) argue that the language that members of a specific community use reflects the values and beliefs that are embedded in their culture and ideologies; in the same way, the culture and dominant ideologies within learning contexts also have a strong impact on the learners' perceptions of the language learning process. In other words, language is a cultural tool which provides the means for members of a group to retain their shared identity and to relate with each other. Through the process of language learning, parents socialize their children into socially and culturally appropriate ways of behaving, speaking, and thinking.

The process of language acquisition for young children is built upon a variety of experiences. From birth, parents and caregivers involve infants in communicative exchanges. These exchanges accompany activities shared by adults and infants, such as bathing, feeding, and dressing. During these activities, parents and caregivers comment on the infants' actions and often repeat and exaggerate their vocalizations (Fernald & Mazzie, 1991). Such communicative exchanges between adults and infants function as a form of social interaction. This social interaction helps build intimacy between adults and infants, enhances infants' interests in their environment, and provides them with stimulation for later language development (Burkato & Daehler, 1995).

The First Year

Crying is the earliest form of infant vocalization. But after only a few weeks of experience with language, infants begin to vocalize in addition to crying: they coo. Infants generally begin to coo at about one month of age (Shaffer, 1999). Cooing is repeating vowel-like sounds such as "oooooh" or "aaaaah." Infants coo when their parents or caregiver interact with them. At around 3 or 4 months, infants start to add consonant sounds to their cooing, and they begin to babble at between 4 and 6 months of age. Babbling consists of consonant and vowel sounds. Infants are able to combine these consonant and vowel sounds into syllable-like sequences, such as mamama, kaka, and dadadada (Berk, 2000; Shaffer, 1999). Through interacting with parents or caregivers by such cooing and babbling, infants develop a sense of the role of language in communication by the end of the first year. The linkage between communication and sound-making signals the onset of true language (Glover & Bruning, 1987).

The Second and Third Year

In the beginning of the second year, children's first words emerge. The first words are also called "holophrases" because children's productive vocabulary usually contains only one or two very simple words at a time, and they seem to utter single words to represent the whole meaning of an entire sentence (Shaffer, 1999). Children's first words are usually very different from adults' speech in terms of the pronunciation, and these first words are most frequently nominals--labels for objects, people, or events (Bukatko & Daehler, 1995). In addition, children's first words are quite contextual. They may use a single word to identify something or somebody under different conditions (such as saying "ma" when seeing mother entering the room), to label objects linked to someone (saying "ma" when seeing mother's lipstick), or to express needs (saying "ma" and extending arms for wanting a hug from the mother). In the initial stage of the first-word utterance, children produce words slowly. However, once they have achieved a productive vocabulary of ten words, children begin to add new words at a faster rate, called "vocabulary spurt" (Barrett, 1985).

By their second birthday, children begin to combine words and to generate simple sentences (Bukatko & Daehler, 1995). Initially, the first sentences are often two-word sentences, gradually evolving into longer ones. Children's first sentences have been called "telegraphic speech" because these sentences resemble the abbreviated language of a telegram. Like the telegram, children's first sentences contain mainly the essential content words, such as verbs and nouns, but omit the function words, such as articles, prepositions, and pronouns, auxiliary verbs (Berk, 2000).

Although children's first sentences seem to be ungrammatical in terms of adult standards, they are far more than strings of random words combined. Instead, they have a structure of their own. A characteristic of the structure is that some words, called "pivot words," are used in a mostly fixed position, and are combined with other less frequently used words referred to as "open words," which can be easily replaced by other words (Braine, 1976). For example, a child may use "more" as a pivot word, and create sentences such as, "more cookie, "more car,"and "more doggie."

Creativity also plays an important role in this first sentence stage. Research has revealed that many of children's early sentences, such as "allgone cookie," and "more read" are creative statements which do not appear in adult speech (Shaffer, 1999). Like the first-word creation, context plays an important role in understanding children's first sentences because both require context in order that understanding can occur. As children's use of simple sentences increases, the amount of single-word use declines, and their sentences become increasingly elaborate and sophisticated. (Glover & Bruning, 1987).

The Preschool Years

By the time children are 3 1/2 to 4 years of age, they have already acquired many important skills in language learning. They have a fairly large working vocabulary and an understanding of the function of words in referring to things and actions. They also have a command of basic conversational skills, such as talking about a variety of topics with different audiences. Nevertheless, language development, especially vocabulary growth and conversational skills, continues (Glover & Bruning, 1987). It is generally agreed that vocabulary learning is not accomplished through formal instruction. Instead, the meaning of new words is usually acquired when children interact with other more skilled language users during such natural situations as riding, eating, and playing (Beals & Tabors, 1995). From these activities, children are able to construct hypotheses when hearing unfamiliar verbal strings. They then test these hypotheses by further observation or by making up new sentences themselves. Finally, through feedback and further exposure, children revise and confirm their hypotheses (Bukatko & Daehler, 1995).

The development of conversational skills also requires children's active interaction with other people. To communicate with others effectively, children need to learn how to negotiate, take turns, and make relevant as well as intelligible contributions (Schickedanz, Schickedanz, Forsyth, & Forsyth, 1998). Through interacting with other more experienced language users, children modify and elaborate their sentences in response to requests for more information (Peterson & McCabe, 1992). As children interact with their playmates, their conversations usually include a series of turn-taking dialogues (Glover & Bruning, 1987). In addition, young children learn to adjust their messages to their listeners' level of understanding (Shatz & Gelman, 1973).

By the time children enter elementary school, their oral language is very similar to that of adults (Shaffer, 1999). They have acquired the basic syntactic, semantic, and pragmatic elements of their native language. Language development will continue, however, from early childhood through adolescence and into adulthood.

Conclusion

In summary, language learning is both a social and a developmental process. To acquire a language, children must interact with other more competent language users as well as explore various aspects of the linguistic system. During the early years of language learning, children also create, test, and revise their hypotheses regarding the use of language. Parents and early childhood educators should provide these young learners with developmentally appropriate language activities, offer opportunities for them to experiment with different aspects of language learning, and honor their creativity.

References

Barrett, M. D. (1985). Issues in the study of children's single word speech. In M. D. Barrett (Ed.), Children's single-word speech. Chichester, England: Wiley.

Beals, D. E., & Tabors, P. O. (1995). Arboretum, bureaucratic and carbohydrate:

Preschoolers' exposure to rare vocabulary at home. First Language, 15, 57-76.
Berk, L. E. (2000). Child development (5th ed.). Boston: Allyn & Bacon.
Braine, M. D. S. (1976). Children's first word combinations. Monographs of the Society for Research in Child Development, 41 (Serial No. 164).
Bukatko, D. & Daehler, M. W. (1995). Child Development: A thematic approach. Boston: Houghton Mifflin Company.
Fernald, A., & Mazzie, C. (1991). Prosody and focus in speech to infants and adults. Developmental Psychology, 27, 209-221.
Glover, J. A. & Bruning, R. H. (1987). Educational Psychology. Boston, MA: Little, Brown & Company.
Muspratt, S., Luke, A., & Freebody, P. (1997). Constructing critical literacies. Cresskill. NJ: Hampton Press.
Peterson, C. & McCabe, A. (1992). Parental styles of narrative elicitation: Effect on children's narrative structure and content. First Language, 12, 299-321.
Schickedanz, J. A., Schickedanz, D. I., Forsyth, P. D., & Forsyth, G. A. (1998). Understanding children and adolescents. (3rd ed). Boston: Allyn and Baon.
Shaffer, D. R. (1999). Developmental psychology: Childhood & adolescence (5th ed.). Pacific Grove, CA: Brook Cole Publishing Company.
Shatz, M. & Gelman, R. (1973). The development of communication skills: Modifications in the speech of young children as a function of listener. Monographs of the Society for Research on Child Development, 38 (Serial No, 152).
Vygotsky, L. S. (1962). Thought and language. (E. Hanfmann & G. Vakar, Eds. & Trans.). Cambridge, MA: MIT Press.

Digest #154 is EDO-CS-00-05 and was published in October 2000 by the ERIC Clearinghouse on Reading, English and Communication, 2805 E 10th Street, Bloomington, IN 47408-2698, Telephone (812) 855-5847 or (800) 759-4723. ERIC Digests are in the public domain and may be freely reproduced. Additional copies may be ordered by contacting the ERIC Document Reproduction Service at (800) 443-3742. This project has been funded at least in part with Federal funds from the U.S. Department of Education under contract number ED-99-CO-0028. The content of this publication does not necessarily reflect the views or policies of the U.S. Department of Education nor does mention of trade names, commercial products, or organizations imply endorsement by the U.S. Government.

Legal Note

All rights reserved. This Study Guide, Book and Flashcards are protected under US Copyright Law. No part of this book or study guide or flashcards may be reproduced, distributed or stored in a retrieval system, or transmitted in any form or by any means, electronic, mechanical, photocopying, recording, or otherwise, without the prior written permission of the publisher Breely Crush Publishing, LLC. This manual is not supported by or affiliated with the College Board, creators of the CLEP test. CLEP is a registered trademark of the College Entrance Examination Board, which does not endorse this book.

All information is copyright of Breely Crush Publishing, LLC except for material contributed by Robert G. Young and James Atherton that is reprinted with permission.

References

[1] ATHERTON J S (2002) Learning and Teaching: Piaget's developmental psychology [On-line]: UK: Available: http://www.dmu.ac.uk/~jamesa/learning/piaget.htm Accessed: 28 March 2003, reprinted with permission.

[2] ATHERTON J S (2002) *Learning and Teaching: Piaget's developmental psychology* [On-line]: UK: Available: http://www.dmu.ac.uk/~jamesa/learning/piaget.htm Accessed: 28 March 2003, reprinted with permission.

[3] ATHERTON J S (2002) *Learning and Teaching: Piaget's developmental psychology* [On-line]: UK: Available: http://www.dmu.ac.uk/~jamesa/learning/piaget.htm Accessed: 28 March 2003, reprinted with permission.

[4] Young, Robert G., http://ryoung001.homestead.com/Freud.html Reprinted with permission.

FLASHCARDS

This section contains flashcards for you to use to further your understanding of the material and test yourself on important concepts, names or dates. Read the term or question then flip the page over to check the answer on the back. Keep in mind that this information may not be covered in the text of the study guide. Take your time to study the flashcards, you will need to know and understand these concepts to pass the test.

Psychoanalyst	Erik Erickson
Most important thing to Erickson	Trust vs. Mistrust
Autonomy vs. Shame and Doubt	Initiative vs. Guilt
Industry vs. Inferiority	Identity vs. Role Confusion

Psychoanalyst	Freud
Infant	Development of trust
Preschooler	Toddler
Adolescent	School-Age

Intimacy vs. Isolation	**Generativity vs. Stagnation**
Ego Integrity vs. Despair	**Jean Piaget**
Accommodation	**Classification**
Class Inclusion	**Conservation**

Middle-Age Adult	Young Adult
Cognitive theorist	Old Age
The ability to group objects together on the basis of common features	The difference made to one's mind or concepts by the process of assimilation
The realization that objects or sets of objects stay the same even when they are changed about or made to look different	The understanding of more advanced than simple classification, that some classes or sets of objects are also sub-sets of a larger class

Developmental Norm	**Egocentrism**
Elaboration	**Operation**
Recognition	**Recall**
Schema	**Stage**

The belief that you are the center of the universe and everything revolves around you	A statistical measure of typical scores for categories of information
The process of working something out in your head	Relating new information to something familiar
Being able to reproduce knowledge from memory	The ability to identify correctly something encountered before
A period in a child's development in which he or she is capable of understanding some things but not others	The representation in the mind of a set of perceptions, ideas, and/or actions, which go together

Reflexive Stage (0-2 months)	**Primary Circular Reactions** (2-4 months)
Secondary Circular Reactions (4-8 months)	**Coordination of Secondary Reactions** (8-12 months)
Tertiary Circular Reactions (12-18 months)	**Invention of New Means Through Mental Combination** (18-24 months)
Preoperational Phase (2-4 years)	**Intuitive Phase** (4-7 years)

Reflexive behaviors occur in stereotyped repetition such as opening and closing fingers repetitively	Simple reflex activity such as grasping and sucking
Responses become coordinated into more complex sequences. Actions take on an "intentional" character	Repetitions of change actions to reproduce interesting consequences such as kicking one's feet to move a mobile suspended over the crib
Evidence of an internal representational system. Symbolizing the problem solving sequence before actually responding. Deferred imitation.	Discovery of new ways to produce the same consequence or obtain the same goal such as the infant may pull a pillow toward him in an attempt to get a toy resting on it.
Speech becomes more social, less egocentric. The child has an intuitive grasp of logical concepts in some areas.	Increased use of verbal representation but speech is egocentric. Transductive reasoning. Can think about something without the object being present by use of language.

Period of Concrete Operations (7-11 years)	**Period of Formal Operations (11-15 years)**
Oral Stage	Anal Stage
Phallic Stage	Latency Stage
Genital Stage	Denial

Thought becomes more abstract, incorporating the principles of formal logic. The ability to generate abstract propositions, multiple hypotheses and their possible outcomes is evident.	Evidence for organized, logical thought. There is the ability to perform multiple classification tasks, order objects in a logical sequence, and comprehend the principle of conservation.
1-3 year	Birth-1 year
6-11 years	3-6 years
Complete rejection of the feeling or situation	Adolescence

Suppression	**Reaction Formation**
Projection	**Displacement**
Rationalization	**Regression**
Sublimation	**Self-actualization**

Turning a feeling into the exact opposite feeling. For example, saying you hate someone you are interested in.	Hiding the feelings and not acknowledging them
Feelings are redirected to someone else. Someone who has a bad day at work and can't complain goes home and yells at their kids instead.	Projection is transferring your thoughts and feelings onto others. For example, someone who is being unfaithful themselves constantly accuses their partner of cheating.
Reverting to old behavior to avoid feelings	You deny your feelings and come up with ways to justify your behavior
Highest need in hierarchy - Level 5	A type of displacement, redirection of the feeling into a socially productive activity

Esteem Needs	**Belonging and Love**
Safety	**Physical Needs**
Operant Conditioning	**Instructional Conditioning**
Extinction	**Egocentric Behavior**

Level 3 need	Level 4 need
Level 1 need	Level 2 need
Gives a negative sanction	Reinforces good behavior
A child does not take into consideration other people's needs	The process of unassociating the condition with the response

Social Learning Theory

Baby Albert

Stimulus Generalization

Naturalistic Observation

Independent Variable

Cross-Sectional Studies

Longitudinal Studies

Quantitative

The kept in a box and conditioned	Explicit role instruction (stereotypes), boys play with trucks and cars, girls wear make-up
Search conducted by watching the subject	Something from conditioning carries over to another related area
When people of different ages are studied at one particular time	The one the researchers have direct control over
The number or amount of something	Where the people are followed over a long period of time and checked up on at certain points

Qualitative	Four Steps of the Scientific Method
Human development begins when?	Prenatal Stage
Infancy to Toddlers	Early Childhood
Middle Childhood	Adolescence

Gather information, generate hypothesis, test hypothesis, revise	Used in statistics, similar in structure or organization
Conception to birth	Fertilization
3-6 years	Birth to 3 years
12-20 years	6-12 years

Young Adulthood	**Middle Adulthood**
Late Adulthood	**Monozygotic Twins**
Dizygotic Twins	**Zygote**
Neonate	**Prenatal Stage**

40-65 years	20-40 years
Identical twins	65+ years
Fertilized egg	Fraternal twins
First three months in the womb	Newborn

Anoxia	How many pairs of chromosomes to a body cell?
How many chromosomes to a body cell total?	Down syndrome cells have how many chromosomes?
At what age does a woman's chance of having a down syndrome baby go way up?	What number is the extra chromosome in a down syndrome baby?
Autism	Rubella

23 pairs	Brain damage caused by failing to breathe
47	46
21	40
German Measles	Lack of responsiveness to other people

Critical Period

Fetal Alcohol syndrome is caused by

Fetal Tobacco syndrome is caused by

Amniocentesis

Medicated Delivery

Gentle Birth

Cesarean Birth

Ferdinand Lamaze

Mother drinking alcohol while pregnant	A time in development when a certain event will have the greatest impact
Sample of the amniotic sac to be tested for various diseases	Mother's smoking while pregnant
Baby is born in a pool or bath with dim lights	Most popular form of delivery
Taught women breathing procedures to get through childbirth	Surgical delivery birth

Anorexia Nervosa	**Bulimia**
STD	**Virginia Apgar rating is used when**
Apgar Ratings Include (5)	**Habituation**
PKU	**Phenylketonuria**

Binge and purge	Self-starvation
At birth	Sexually transmitted diseases
To get used to something	Appearance, pulse, grimace, activity, respiration
PKU	Enzyme Deficiency

SIDS	**Visual Cliff**
Object Permanence	**Harry Harlow**
Who made the first IQ test?	**Formula to find out IQ?**
Hyperactivity affects what percentage of children?	**Divergent Thinking**

Experiment to prove infants have depth perception	Sudden Infant Death Syndrome
Monkey experiment - monkeys liked the soft one better	Understanding that an object does not cease to exist once it has left your vision
IQ=Mental Age/Calculated Age x 100	Alfred Binet
Creative process of thinking	0.03

Convergent Thinking	**Nature vs. Nurture**
Four Stages of Speech	**Echolalia**
Id	**Ego**
Super Ego	**Kibbutz**

Are personalities determined by biology or environment	Follower thinking
When a baby repeats what you just said	Cooing, babbling, hollow phrases, telegraphic speech
The mediator between ego and id	Primitive part of the subconscious which wants food and sex
Commune where children are raised by all	Ethical, super good part of the subconscious

Kohlberg's Theory of Moral Development

Preconventional Morality

Conventional Morality

Postconventional Morality

Hurried Child

Resilient Child

Rite of Passage

Psychometrics

Punishment of obedience phase	How morality is linked to behavior
Motivation is because law is a higher order	Motivation to obey is done from influence of other people
A child that bounces back from difficult situations	A rushed child
Cultural bias not generally known across all subcultures	An event that shows maturation of a child

Mainstreaming	**Self-concept**
Deferred Imitation	**Gender Conservation**
Authoritarian	**Permissive**
Authoritative	**Teratogens**

Who am I?	Mixing non-mainstreaming kids with mainstream ones
Realization that a child's gender will stay the same	Imitation of a passed observed behavior
Few demands	Because I say so
Substances which are harmful to prenatal development	Respects individuality

Gerontology

Ageism

Presbycusis

Autonomy

Inferiority

Generativity

Integrity

Piaget believed that the transition of children's thinking took place when?

When people who are working experience discrimination because of their age, regardless of if they are considered too old or too young.	The study of the aging process.
When the parents give the child the necessary free reign over their choices.	The loss of hearing that occurs with aging.
Leaving something for the next generation.	Develops from negative social situations.
18 months, 7 years, and 11 or 12 years.	Comes from achieving what one wanted in life.

Cognitive theorist	Assimiliation
Decentration	Transductive reasoning
Formal logic	What did Piaget and Freud both agree about environmental influences?
Oedipus conflict	Electra conflict

The process by which a person takes material in their mind from the environment, which may mean changing the evidence of their senses to make it fit.	Believes that the individual actively constructs knowledge about the world.
To figure that two unrelated instances are connected, without inductive or deductive reasoning.	The move away from egocentrism.
They can affect the time spent in stages but not the order.	Making deductions that seem self-evident.
Girls feel a sexual desire for the other-sex parent.	Boys feel a sexual desire for the other-sex parent.

Oral stage (birth-1 year)

Anal stage (1-3 years)

Phallic stage (3-6 years)

Latency stage (6-11 years)

Genital adolescence

Defense mechanisms

Classical conditioning

Reinforcer

Young toddlers and preschoolers enjoy holding and releasing urine and feces.	Baby's sucking activities directed toward breast or bottle, and if needs not met, may develop habits such as thumb sucking, fingernail biting, pencil chewing, overeating, and smoking.
Sexual instincts die down and the super ego develops further.	Impulses transfer to the genitals, and the child finds pleasure in genital stimulation.
Things that help us relieve stress.	Sexual impulses of the phallic stage reappear.
Anything which makes a behavior more likely to reoccur.	Describes a link between a stimulus and a response in which a person or animal associates or substitutes a neutral stimulus with the actual stimulus.

| Positive reinforcer | Negative reinforcer |

| Punishments | Extrinsic reinforcer |

| Intrinsic reinforcer | Response extinction |

| Modeling | Telegraphic speech |

When something unpleasant is removed from a situation.	When something pleasant is used to make a behavior more likely.
Something physical or from the environment.	Conditioning that can attempt to make a behavior less likely to reoccur.
A method of modifying behavior in which you ignore the behavior so you don't have the response.	Something which comes from within the individual or something emotional.
A speech pattern in which a person eliminates function words from their sentences, instead keeping only the important content words.	People pattern their behavior off of others who they find admirable or similar to themselves.

Fast mapping

Language acquisition

Case study

Survey

Self-report data

Laboratory observation

Correlation research

Correlation coefficient

When children are learning new words.	The process through which new words and concepts are learned after a single exposure.
A great way to get information about a specific type of information. Usually, questionnaires are given out to participants who are then asked to answer questions to the best of their ability.	A single individual (subject) is intensely studied.
Observation conducted in a laboratory environment to monitor specific biological changes in individuals.	When a participant fills out a survey themselves about themselves.
Measures the strength between two variables.	Used to show links between events, people, actions, behaviors, etc.

Positive correlation	Negative correlation
A correlation of zero shows what?	Census
Sample	Bias
Informed consent	Dependent variable

When one variable increases, the other variable decreases.	When one variable increases, the other variable increases as well.
A collection of data from all cases or people in the chosen set.	There is no relationship between variables.
The distortion of results.	A set of cases of people randomly chosen from a large group.
All other variables other than the independent variable.	The participants must know the content of the experiment and be warned of any risk or harm.

Mean	**Median**
Mode	**Cephalocaudal**
Proximodistal	**Cerebral anoxia**
Mentally retarded	**Myelin**

Middle number in a set of data.	Average
Growth from the head downward during the embryonic period.	The number which occurs the most often.
A lack of oxygen to the brain.	Growth from the center (or spine) outward during the embryonic period.
Insulation for nerves.	Low IQ and a mental age of about 4 years old.

Teratology	**Teratogens**
Attachment theory	**Semantics**
Holophrase syntax	**Morphemes**
Bound morpheme	**Free morpheme**

Harmful substances.	The study of substances which are harmful to prenatal development.
The scientific study of words and sentences.	Infants need to form at least one strong attachment, such as to a parent, in order to develop normally.
The smallest unit of a word which has meaning.	A communication style in which single words are used to communicate.
Can be a word on its own.	Must be with a word.

Phonemes	English has how many phonemes?
School phobia	Childhood depression
Psychological maltreatment	Self-esteem
Peer group	Momentary playmates stage of friendship

40	The individual sounds.
Similar to adult depression and usually exhibited as "nobody likes me."	Dread of school.
Begins in middle childhood.	Not physical abuse, but when the child feels rejected or feels failure.
Ages 3-7	The other students in the environment where children live and attend school.

NOTES

NOTES